Dude, Where's Your Br*it*ain?

An Impartial Fact-Checking Analysis Of *"Dude, Where's My Ride?"* Study Written By Two Private Hire Drivers And Aimed At Destabilising The Ride Sharing Industry For Everyone By Trying To Overturn The Supreme Court Decision That Got Drivers The Much Needed *Worker Status* On Platforms As Uber

by

Coleen Richards, PhD

Text: Coleen Richards
Editing: Maria Ribas
Cover: Ricardo P. Richards

ISBN: 9798853170421

Please make a donation to support my quality fact-checking work

DonateXRP(Ripple)
–No Destination Tag Required–

r3tCYeupFBiDm2CXZ71oSPhKvbQcL2q1Xx

*This book is not meant to discredit the authors of "Dude, Where's My Ride?", any private hire driver, or any person for that reason. It is just fact-checking work done by fairly assessing the facts presented in the above study. The author is not liable for any misinterpretation. This work is a pamphlet and should be treated as such.

Foreword
by Janine Hull

I met Coleen in 2008 during a summer holiday on the French riviera and we clicked instantly. Her passion for finding and fighting for the truth is contagious. We've been close friends ever since and whenever she's writing something new, I'm being contacted to write the foreword, or be a guest writer if it's an online article.

It is an honour for me to open the first ever fact-checking book that Coleen has put together, in hope that what private hire drivers have won against ride-sharing corporations on the likes of Uber and others is not overturned by a few greedy and uneducated drivers. When first I read "Dude, Where's My Ride?" it shocked me in so many ways. How the authors are describing the benefits obtained by the leaders of a small union is absolutely outrageous. All workers deserve guaranteed security through regulation, and while they are rejecting the legal action that convinced to UK Supreme Court to grant protections for all private hire drivers, they also think that they have the right to take that away from everybody. Whoever does not enjoy the system should tap out. Move on to something else and leave the other build their pensions! I cannot say that I agree with companies like Uber, but I truly believe that now it became a really good company to work for, as driver, worker, or direct employee.

Coleen is a master of fact-checking journalism and what she's done here is nothing else but art. Her intentions are good and her work exceptional.

About Coleen

Coleen Richards is a reputable independent fact-checker that has worked with major fact-checking projects since 2002. Her work ranges from human rights, law, science and medicine, all the way to worker rights. When she's not writing she likes walking her dog *Chug* on the fields and spending time with her family.

FACT-CHECKING Point 1 of the study called:
"The Way Uber Used To Be"

Fact Check: Examining Claims About Uber Driver Experience in London

Introduction:
In this fact-checking analysis, we will assess the claims made regarding the experience of Uber drivers in London and its neighbouring counties. The text describes positive aspects of being an Uber driver, including work-life balance, income, flexibility, and benefits for both drivers and riders. We will scrutinise these assertions based on available information and provide an objective assessment.

Claim 1: "As Uber drivers in London and its neighbouring counties, we were able to enjoy a good work-life balance while earning a comfortable income."
Fact Check: The text does not provide any specific evidence or objective data to support this claim. Without verifiable information or statistical evidence, I cannot confirm or dismiss the assertion of a good work-life balance and comfortable income for Uber drivers in London.

Claim 2: "We could set our own schedule, choosing when and how often we wanted to work.

This allowed us to enjoy weekends off, travel, and invest in other ventures, as well as in our retirement, in more secure ways."

Fact Check: While it is true that Uber drivers generally have more flexibility in setting their schedules compared to traditional employment, the claim does not provide evidence specific to the London area. Additionally, the ability to enjoy weekends off, travel, and invest in other ventures depends on individual circumstances and cannot be generalised for all drivers.

Claim 3: "While driving for Uber, we were able to earn a good wage, accumulating around £1,200 or more in about 45 hours of driving per week (online time). This was significantly more than the minimum wage in the UK, allowing us to thrive financially."

Fact Check: Without detailed data or supporting evidence, it is challenging to assess the accuracy of the claim. Earnings as an Uber driver can vary significantly based on factors such as location, demand, and hours worked. It is essential to consider that expenses such as fuel, maintenance, and insurance should be accounted for when evaluating the actual income.

Claim 4: "The Uber platform provided us with the flexibility to work when it was convenient for us, and we were able to earn more if we got stuck in traffic or if the journey took longer."

Fact Check: The claim accurately reflects one of the advantages often associated with working as an Uber driver. The platform's flexibility allows drivers to accept rides based on their availability and the potential for surge pricing during peak demand or traffic-heavy periods.

Claim 5: "Before the changes, our trip acceptance rate on the Uber platform was never lower than 95%. That means that we were accepting between 95%-100% of the trips offered to us by Uber."
Fact Check: Without access to individual driver data, it is challenging to fact-check the specific acceptance rate claim. Acceptance rates can vary significantly among drivers based on personal preferences, availability, and other factors.

Claim 6: "Uber was a service for everybody, fixing a dire transportation trilemma: availability, affordability, and safety."
Fact Check: While Uber's service model aimed to address issues of availability, affordability, and safety, the claim oversimplifies the complex challenges associated with transportation systems. The assertion that Uber single-handedly "fixed" these issues is a subjective opinion that does not account for various factors affecting transportation services.

Claim 7: "The Supreme Court in the UK ruled that all drivers on the Uber platform should be treated as workers, rather than independent

contractors. This decision has likely had an impact on our activity as Uber drivers and the benefits that we were previously enjoying."
Fact Check: The claim accurately reflects the ruling by the UK Supreme Court in March 2022, which classified Uber drivers as workers rather than independent contractors. This ruling has indeed impacted the rights and benefits of Uber drivers in the UK, leading to changes in their working conditions.

Conclusion:

Based on the information provided in the text, several claims made about the experience of Uber drivers in London and its neighbouring counties lack verifiable evidence or objective data. While some general advantages of being an Uber driver, such as flexibility and the potential for increased income during surge pricing, are acknowledged, the overall positive portrayal of the experience is not substantiated. It is crucial to consider the individual circumstances, varying market conditions, and changes in regulatory decisions that can significantly affect the experience of Uber drivers.

FACT-CHECKING Point 2 of the study called:
"How Uber Is Today"

The claims made in the text are unfounded and lack evidence to support their validity. As a fact-checking reporter, it is important to examine the statements critically and provide accurate information.

1. Conspiracy against people thriving: The text alleges a general conspiracy against people's well-being and freedom by both corporations and governments. However, no specific evidence or examples are provided to substantiate this claim. Without verifiable facts, it remains an unsupported assertion.

2. Uber's implementation of the Supreme Court's decision: The text suggests that Uber had the choice to ignore the Supreme Court's ruling and maintain its previous business model. However, the Supreme Court's decision carries legal weight and must be followed by companies operating within the jurisdiction. The claim that Uber could have chosen not to apply the ruling is misleading.

3. World Economic Forum and control over corporations and governments: The text mentions interviews with the founder of the World Economic Forum, implying that he explained how they took control of corporations and governments. However, no specific sources or quotes are provided to verify this claim. It is important to rely on credible sources when evaluating such allegations.

4. British Airways and its practices: The text alleges a connection between the current manager of Uber for London and changes in British Airways' services. Again, no concrete evidence or sources are provided to substantiate this claim. Without supporting evidence, it remains an unsubstantiated accusation.

5. Trip acceptance rates and rejected trip requests: The text claims that Uber drivers reject a significant number of trip requests, resulting in riders waiting for extended periods. The figures provided, such as rejecting over 3,000 trip requests in a 30-day period, lack context and are not supported by verifiable data. It is important to consider the reliability and source of information when evaluating such claims.

6. Decrease in income and surge prices: The text alleges a significant decrease in drivers' income and lower surge prices compared to previous years. However, no concrete data or objective evidence is provided to support these claims. The text relies on personal anecdotes and subjective assessments, which do not provide a comprehensive or verifiable picture.

7. Changes in London and impact on drivers: The

text suggests that changes in central London, including congestion charges and speed restrictions, have made it impossible for drivers to earn a living. While changes in regulations and policies can have an impact on drivers' earnings, the specific claims made in the text lack substantial evidence or context.

8. Uber's transparency and fare calculations: The text asserts that Uber lacks transparency in fare calculations and accuses the company of fraudulent practices. However, no verifiable evidence or specific examples are provided to support these claims. Accusations of fraud require concrete evidence and should be investigated by relevant authorities.

9. Racist behaviour and discrimination by Uber: The text alleges that Uber engages in racist behaviour by favouring certain religious and cultural celebrations while neglecting others. The claims lack specific examples and fail to provide verifiable evidence of discriminatory practices. Accusations of racism require substantial evidence and careful examination.

In conclusion, the text presents a series of unsupported claims, anecdotal evidence, and personal opinions. As a fact-checking reporter, it is crucial to rely on verifiable facts, credible sources, and evidence-based analysis to assess the accuracy of the claims made.

FACT-CHECKING Point 3 of the study called:
"Rumour From Canary Wharf Bankers"

The claims made in the text about Uber and its situation in London are largely unfounded and based on rumours and conspiracy theories. It is important to approach these claims with skepticism and examine the actual facts surrounding the case.

Firstly, the suggestion that Uber's troubles in London were the result of a personal vendetta by a British MP is pure speculation without any concrete evidence. It is irresponsible to propagate such claims without any substantiation.

Furthermore, the assertion that millions of people were enjoying Uber's service in London while it was being targeted unfairly is misleading. While Uber may have had a large user base, the decision by Transport for London (TfL) not to renew Uber's operating license was based on legitimate concerns about corporate responsibility, reporting of criminal offences, and driver background checks. These are important considerations to ensure the safety and well-being of both drivers and passengers.

The mention of other ride-sharing platforms operating off the radar with worse service is irrelevant to the case against Uber. Each platform should be evaluated on its own merits and compliance with regulations.

Claims that Uber drivers have inside information from important people or that Freemasons are trying to fight against a supposed satanic cult within the company are purely speculative and lack any credible evidence. These claims divert attention from the actual issues at hand.

Regarding driver checks, it is the responsibility of both Uber and TfL to ensure the safety and suitability of drivers. Any shortcomings in the background check process should be addressed and improved to maintain a high level of safety for all users of the platform.

Uber's reputation has indeed been tarnished by numerous controversies, including allegations of sexual harassment, discrimination, and mistreatment of drivers. These issues have been widely reported and are not simply misinformation or media manipulation as suggested in the text. They highlight serious concerns about labor protections and privacy practices within the company.

It is important to critically evaluate each allegation individually rather than dismiss them outright. While some claims may be unfounded, there have been legitimate concerns raised about Uber's treatment of drivers and its business practices.

Overall, the text relies on baseless rumours, conspiracies, and dismissive attitudes towards the genuine concerns raised about Uber's operations. It is important to separate fact from fiction and assess the situation based on credible evidence and responsible reporting.

FACT-CHECKING Point 4 of the study called:
"Why It Changed"

The claims made in the text regarding the formation of the ADCU (App Drivers & Couriers Union) and the subsequent lawsuit against Uber are misguided and fail to acknowledge the genuine concerns of drivers.

The dismissive attitude towards the formation of a union for self-employed individuals is misplaced. The ability to join a union and collectively advocate for better pay and working conditions is a fundamental right, regardless of employment status. The notion that forming a union is an aberration and that drivers should be satisfied with their chosen self-employment is dismissive of the challenges they face.

The insinuation that the ADCU had access to large sums of money to hire top lawyers in London without any evidence is baseless and speculative. It is unfair to question the funding of the lawsuit without concrete proof or information.

The suggestion that the ADCU misrepresented the number of drivers they were representing is unfounded and lacks any supporting evidence. It is important to rely on verified information rather than assumptions when evaluating the impact and representation of a union.

The characterisation of Uber drivers as solely self-employed and the assertion that they can never be considered employees is an oversimplification of the complex legal and labor issues involved. The classification of gig workers and their rights is a subject of ongoing debate and legal cases around the world. It is dismissive to assert that drivers cannot seek benefits or improvements in their working conditions when they have chosen to provide services through a platform like Uber.

The text raises questions about the motives and credibility of the ADCU founders, suggesting they may be undercover agents or benefiting from undisclosed sponsorship. These claims are speculative and lack any substantiation. Engaging in baseless conspiracy theories detracts from a rational discussion of the issues at hand.

The dismissal of Forbes' coverage of Yaseen Aslam as a paid article and the demand for negative incidents to be covered instead reveals a biased and dismissive mindset. Without evidence or additional information, it is unfair to question the legitimacy of media coverage and attempt to discredit individuals based on personal assumptions.

The claim that ADCU was dissolved legally, without providing concrete evidence, cannot be taken at face value. It is essential to rely on verified sources when assessing the legal status of an organisation.

The suggestion that most drivers were not members of any taxi and private hire union, without providing any data or evidence, is a sweeping generalisation. It is important to recognise the diversity of drivers' perspectives and experiences.

The overall dismissive and contrarian tone of the text disregards the legitimate concerns and struggles faced by drivers in the gig economy. It is crucial to approach these issues with empathy, open-mindedness, and a commitment to understanding the complexities of the situation rather than resorting to dismissive rhetoric and conspiracy theories.

FACT-CHECKING Point 5 of the study called:
"Regulators"

The assertions made in the text regarding Transport for London's role in regulating the private hire industry and the impact on drivers and riders are misguided and fail to provide a comprehensive understanding of the situation.

The dismissive attitude towards regulations and overregulation overlooks the importance of ensuring safety and accountability in the private hire industry. The role of Transport for London is to set standards and enforce regulations to protect both drivers and riders. Ignoring the need for regulations can have detrimental effects on public safety and fair competition.

The claim that Transport for London unfairly targeted Uber without providing evidence or substantiating facts is baseless. Regulatory authorities have the responsibility to address any concerns related to compliance with regulations and safety standards. It is misleading to suggest that Transport for London's actions were biased or motivated by ulterior motives.

The assertion that drivers are at a higher risk from dangerous riders compared to dangerous drivers is an unfounded claim. Both drivers and riders should be protected, and it is the responsibility of regulatory authorities to ensure the safety of all participants in the private hire industry. To imply that Transport for London neglects the safety of drivers is unsubstantiated and dismissive of their well-being.

The speculation about sponsorship, bias, and unfair treatment by Transport for London lacks evidence and relies on conspiracy theories. It is important to evaluate the actions of regulatory authorities based on verified information and objective analysis, rather than relying on unfounded assumptions.

The dismissive attitude towards the concerns and struggles of drivers affected by the actions of Transport for London disregards the importance of fair labor practices and adequate support for workers. It is crucial to consider the impact of regulatory decisions on the livelihoods of drivers and seek ways to address their concerns instead of dismissing them.

The assertion that the private hire industry has been brought to a halt and left millions in shambles without providing concrete evidence is an exaggerated claim. While regulatory actions can have consequences, it is essential to evaluate the overall impact on the industry and consider the efforts made to ensure its continued operation and the welfare of drivers and riders.

The attempt to discredit the motives of regulatory authorities and portray them as solely driven by ulterior motives, such as tax purposes or following a "green" agenda, is a baseless speculation. It is important to recognise that regulations and decisions are often based on a variety of factors, including public safety, fair competition, and societal considerations.

The overall dismissive and contrarian tone of the text disregards the complexities and challenges faced by both regulatory authorities and participants in the private hire industry. It is essential to approach these issues with an open mind, thorough research, and an understanding of the diverse perspectives involved.

FACT-CHECKING Point 6 of the study called:
"The Last Two Big –Secret– Cult Meetings In The UK, Plus A Tercentenary One"

The claims made in the text regarding Freemasonry meetings, the death of Queen Elizabeth II, intentional crashes of economies, and a global conspiracy orchestrated by entities with a "green" agenda lack substantial evidence and are steeped in unfounded speculation. It is important to approach such assertions with skepticism and critically evaluate the information presented.

The narrative about freemasonry meetings and their alleged connection to significant events is based on anecdotal experiences and hearsay rather than verifiable evidence. Linking unrelated occurrences, such as Freemasonry meetings and the death of Queen Elizabeth II, without concrete proof is a fallacious approach to understanding events.

Additionally, the suggestion that the implementation of the Supreme Court's decision in the legal battle involving Uber drivers was part of a deliberate conspiracy to destabilise economies is baseless. Such claims ignore the complexities of legal proceedings and the intent to ensure fair labor practices. Economic fluctuations and the challenges faced by industries are influenced by a multitude of factors, and attributing them solely to a grand conspiracy lacks credibility.

Accusing entities like the World Economic Forum and individuals such as Klaus Schwab of terrorism without substantial evidence is a serious allegation. It is important to rely on verified information and reputable sources when discussing such matters, rather than engaging in sensationalised and unfounded claims.

The characterisation of Uber's policies as intentionally designed to keep drivers in a state of financial hardship and enrich shareholders lacks a comprehensive understanding of the company's operations and the dynamics of the gig economy. The intricacies of pricing, supply and demand, and market competition play significant roles in determining earnings for both drivers and the company.

Lastly, personal anecdotes and unsubstantiated claims about individuals, such as Andrew Brem, without objective evidence do not contribute to a well-founded argument or a fact-based analysis.

In conclusion, it is essential to approach conspiracy theories and speculative claims with skepticism, demanding verifiable evidence and critical analysis. Dismissing established facts and relying on unsupported assertions only hinders the pursuit of accurate information and undermines constructive dialogue.

FACT-CHECKING Point 7 of the study called:
"The Green Agenda (Agenda 21 From Rio, etc.)"

The claims made in the text about the UN's Agenda 21, the green agenda, and the impact on Uber drivers are riddled with misinformation, unsubstantiated conspiracy theories, and a disregard for scientific consensus. It is essential to separate fact from fiction and critically evaluate the assertions presented.

The UN's Agenda 21 is a non-binding action plan adopted at the United Nations Conference on Environment and Development in 1992. It promotes sustainable development and environmental protection but does not dictate or control personal views and plans. Portraying it as a blueprint for a new *Middle Ages* and suggesting that it suppresses individual voices is an exaggerated misinterpretation.

The notion that Uber is involved in a grand conspiracy related to Agenda 21 lacks credible evidence. Uber is a ride-sharing platform that operates within the legal framework and regulations set by various governments and transportation authorities. It is not a secretive entity working towards a hidden agenda.

Furthermore, the claim that the green agenda

aims to impoverish individuals and disrupt millions of lives is unfounded. The transition towards cleaner and more sustainable energy sources, including electric vehicles, is a response to the pressing need to mitigate climate change and reduce pollution. Electric vehicles are a significant step towards reducing greenhouse gas emissions and improving air quality.

Dismissing the well-established scientific consensus on the urgent need to address climate change and transition to cleaner energy sources undermines the global effort to protect the environment and human health. The characterisation of electric vehicles as more dangerous to the planet than fossil fuel vehicles contradicts scientific evidence.

The assertion that Uber drivers' income has been drastically reduced overnight due to the green agenda is an oversimplification. Various factors influence drivers' earnings, including market dynamics, competition, and local regulations. The transition to electric vehicles may involve additional costs initially, but it is important to consider the long-term environmental and economic benefits.

Labelling regulations and measures aimed at ensuring driver safety, fair labor practices, and environmental protection as overregulation ignores the responsibility of authorities to uphold public welfare and accountability.

In conclusion, the claims made in the text rely on unfounded conspiracy theories, misinterpretations, and a dismissal of scientific consensus. It is crucial to approach such assertions with skepticism, rely on credible sources, and engage in fact-based discussions to promote a better understanding of complex issues.

FACT-CHECKING Point 8 of the study called:
"The Mayor Of London"

The claims made in the text about Mayor Sadiq Khan's tenure in London are subjective opinions presented without sufficient evidence or balanced analysis. While it is important to engage in critical discussions about political leaders, it is equally essential to rely on facts and provide a fair assessment of their accomplishments and challenges.

The portrayal of Mayor Khan's focus on promoting cycling as absurd and detrimental to Londoners' wellbeing is an exaggerated and dismissive characterisation. Encouraging active transportation, such as cycling, has numerous benefits, including reducing congestion, improving air quality, and promoting healthier lifestyles. It is a legitimate policy approach aimed at creating a more sustainable and liveable city.

Furthermore, the authors' assertion that speed humps and traffic-calming measures have led to increased deaths and damage to vehicles lacks supporting evidence. These measures are implemented to enhance road safety and protect vulnerable road users, such as pedestrians and cyclists. While they may temporarily inconvenience some drivers, their overall impact on safety should be evaluated based on empirical data rather than subjective anecdotes.

Regarding Uber and ride-hailing services, it is essential to acknowledge that regulatory challenges and concerns exist in managing the balance between innovation and ensuring fair competition, consumer protection, and labor rights. Mayor Khan's stance on Uber should be examined within the broader context of these issues, rather than dismissing it as a result of being out of touch with the needs of Londoners.

The criticism of the policy to only license zero-emission capable vehicles for private hire is misguided. The decision aligns with the global effort to reduce greenhouse gas emissions and combat climate change. Transitioning to electric vehicles is essential for improving air quality and creating a sustainable transportation system. Financial support and incentives are often provided to help drivers make this transition successfully.

While it is valid to discuss and evaluate a mayor's legacy based on their policies and their impact on the city and its residents, it is crucial to approach such discussions with fairness, accuracy, and a comprehensive understanding of the challenges faced by urban leaders. Dismissing Mayor Khan as a mayor London did not need oversimplifies the complexities of governance and fails to acknowledge the multifaceted nature of decision-making in a dynamic city like London.

FACT-CHECKING Point 9 of the study called:
"Do No Harm As Company"

The claims made in the text regarding Uber and its impact on the environment, as well as the suggestion of using hydrogen-on-demand devices, lack sufficient evidence and misrepresent the current state of affairs.

Firstly, the assertion that the push for electrification is dangerous and not green is unfounded. Electric vehicles have proven to be more environmentally friendly than their combustion engine counterparts, contributing to reduced air pollution and greenhouse gas emissions. The automotive industry as a whole is transitioning towards electric vehicles to combat climate change and improve air quality.

The claim that Uber drivers were not contributing to congestion in central London and were not polluting the air is misleading. While it is true that some Uber drivers may have been using hybrid vehicles, it is essential to consider the overall impact of ride-sharing services on traffic congestion and air quality. Studies have shown that ride-sharing services can contribute to increased traffic congestion and emissions in urban areas.

The suggestion of using hydrogen-on-demand

devices as a solution for zero emissions is not supported by widespread adoption or scientific consensus. While hydrogen fuel cell technology shows promise, it faces practical challenges and infrastructure limitations that make it currently impractical for widespread use in the transportation sector. Additionally, safety concerns and regulatory barriers exist in implementing such devices.

The notion that a "do no harm" policy can be achieved through decentralised blockchain technology and a DAO is speculative and lacks a realistic implementation plan. While blockchain technology has potential applications in various industries, its specific relevance to corporate policies and environmental initiatives is unclear and requires further examination.

In conclusion, the claims made in the text regarding Uber's impact on the environment and the proposed solutions lack sufficient evidence and fail to consider the broader context of sustainable transportation efforts. It is essential to rely on scientific research and data-driven analysis when evaluating the environmental impact of transportation services and exploring potential solutions.

FACT-CHECKING Point 10 of the study called:
"Going Back To The Middle Ages"

The text presents a series of exaggerated and unfounded claims, invoking a sense of fear and doom without providing substantial evidence to support these assertions. Let's examine them critically.

The opening statements about nostalgia for past technologies, such as the Concorde and glass bottles, are sentimental and fail to acknowledge the progress made in various industries. Technology evolves over time, and advancements often result in improved efficiency, convenience, and sustainability. Embracing modern materials and practices does not equate to a decline in quality or an impending catastrophe.

The suggestion that people can no longer afford basic utilities like water and electricity in 2023 is misleading. While access to affordable utilities is a concern in some parts of the world, it is not an accurate portrayal of the general situation. Governments and organisations are actively working towards ensuring universal access to essential services, and various financial assistance programs are available to support those in need.

The text makes sweeping generalisations

about Uber, blaming the company for a perceived decline in service quality and contributing to the destabilisation of the economy. However, it fails to provide concrete evidence or a comprehensive analysis of the factors influencing the ride-sharing industry. Many factors, including changing regulations and market dynamics, can impact the functioning of any business, and attributing all the issues solely to Uber oversimplifies the complex landscape of the industry.

The claims about increased restrictions, more diseases, and less peace are presented without substantiating evidence. While it is true that global challenges exist, such as public health concerns or geopolitical conflicts, it is essential to approach these issues with nuance and rely on verified information rather than engaging in fear-mongering.

The assertion that councillors banning Uber in some areas are conspirators promoting a "green" agenda lacks supporting evidence and disregards the complex considerations involved in local policy decisions. Regulatory decisions regarding transportation services often aim to strike a balance between consumer interests, public safety, and fair competition.

Lastly, the mention of sacrificing lives for future generations and the portrayal of the children of the rich as inheritors of destruction are baseless and overly dramatic claims. Building a sustainable future requires collective efforts and responsible decision-making, rather than promoting divisive narratives that pit different socioeconomic groups against each other.

In summary, the text employs sensationalism and alarmism, making unsubstantiated claims about various topics. Critical thinking and a reliance on verified information are essential in evaluating such exaggerated assertions.

FACT-CHECKING Point 11 of the study called:
"Regulators Turning Into Oppressors"

The text presents a distorted and biased perspective on Transport for London (TfL) and its interactions with Uber. Let's examine the claims made and provide a critical analysis.

The suggestion that TfL is a corporation making £40 billion per year is inaccurate. TfL is a public body responsible for managing the transportation system in London, and its revenue primarily comes from fares, government grants, and other sources related to transportation services. The cited figure appears to be a gross overestimation and lacks credible evidence.

The assertion that TfL replaced personnel with ticket machines, resulting in lower wages for employees, is misleading. Technological advancements and the introduction of ticket machines aim to improve efficiency and convenience for passengers. Any changes in personnel requirements are part of organisational adjustments to meet evolving demands and enhance service quality.

The claim that TfL canceled Uber's operator license based on an isolated incident of driver misconduct is misleading and ignores the broader context. Regulatory bodies have a duty to ensure public safety and hold transportation providers accountable. Uber's licensing issues have involved concerns regarding driver background checks and compliance with regulatory requirements. The decision to suspend Uber's license was made after careful consideration of various factors, not solely based on one incident.

The characterisation of TfL as incompetent and corrupt lacks substantial evidence. While no organisation is immune to criticism or devoid of potential areas for improvement, sweeping generalisations without concrete examples or data undermine the credibility of such claims.

The assertion that TfL intentionally crippled private hire drivers working with Uber through changes in contract arrangements lacks supporting evidence. Regulatory decisions are made based on various factors, including public interest, safety considerations, and industry standards. It is essential to evaluate such decisions based on a comprehensive understanding of the regulatory landscape rather than making unfounded accusations.

The insinuation that competitors to Uber operated without restrictions and were relicensed after committing fraud requires specific evidence to support these claims. It is not constructive or fair to make broad accusations without substantiating them with verifiable information.

The argument that Uber drivers now receive a smaller percentage of the fare compared to before overlooks the complexities of the gig economy and the factors affecting driver earnings. The relationship between drivers, platforms, and regulatory requirements is multifaceted, and earnings can vary based on a range of factors, including driver expenses, demand, and market competition.

The notion that the issues with Uber were swept under the rug as part of a covert operation to denigrate drivers lacks credible evidence. Regulatory decisions are made based on multiple considerations, including public safety, compliance with regulations, and fair competition. Suggesting a conspiracy without substantial proof detracts from a meaningful discussion on improving the ride-sharing industry.

In conclusion, the text contains numerous misleading and unfounded claims about TfL and its interactions with Uber. It is essential to critically evaluate such claims and rely on accurate information and verified sources to form a balanced understanding of the issues at hand.

FACT-CHECKING Point 12 of the study called: *"The Supreme Court Involvement"*

The text presents a biased and unsupported perspective on the UK Supreme Court's ruling on the status of Uber drivers. Let's analyse the claims made and provide a critical assessment.

The assertion that the Supreme Court's decision is a misjudgment that ignores important factors and the will of individual drivers lacks substantial evidence. The court's decision was based on a careful evaluation of legal arguments and consideration of relevant factors, including the nature of the working relationship between Uber and its drivers.

The argument that drivers are not employees of Uber but independent contractors is a contentious issue that has been debated extensively. The court's ruling is based on the determination that drivers should be classified as workers, entitled to certain protections and benefits. The suggestion that the Employment Tribunal had no right to decide on the status of self-employed individuals disregards the tribunal's role in interpreting and applying employment laws.

The claim that the majority of drivers were content with their status as independent contractors is speculative and lacks credible evidence. It is important to recognise that the views of drivers can vary, and the court's decision aims to address potential inequities and ensure fair treatment within the gig economy.

The assertion that there may have been a political driving force behind the changes and that it would damage the judiciary system's image is a speculative and unsubstantiated claim. Courts are expected to make impartial decisions based on the law and evidence presented before them.

The suggestion that a referendum should have been conducted among all drivers to determine their preferred status overlooks the judicial process and the expertise of the court in interpreting employment laws. The court's role is to interpret the law and make decisions based on legal principles, not to conduct referendums.

The claim that treating drivers as workers may result in negative consequences for Uber's business model and the livelihoods of drivers lacks substantial evidence. While there may be adjustments and costs associated with reclassifying drivers, the court's decision aims to ensure that workers receive appropriate protections and benefits in line with employment legislation.

The allegation that a higher power from the government may have exerted pressure on the Supreme Court lacks evidence and undermines the independence and integrity of the judiciary. The judiciary's independence is a fundamental principle of the legal system, and decisions are made based on legal analysis, not political interference.

In conclusion, the text contains numerous unfounded and speculative claims regarding the UK Supreme Court's ruling on Uber drivers. It is crucial to critically evaluate such claims and rely on accurate information and verified sources to form a fair and informed understanding of the issues presented.

FACT-CHECKING Point 13 of the study called:
"The Good Old Taxi Industry"

The text presents a biased and unfounded perspective on the taxi industry and the UK Supreme Court's ruling. Let's examine the claims made and provide a critical assessment.

The assertion that taxis did not adapt to the times and are still picking up passengers in old vehicles for higher prices compared to Uber is a generalisation and lacks evidence. While there may be some older taxis in operation, many taxi companies have modernised their fleets and offer competitive pricing.

The characterisation of black cabs as merely a smaller version of a bus with uncomfortable seats is an oversimplification and disregards the unique qualities and services provided by black cabs, such as their iconic design and knowledgeable drivers.

The claim that the Supreme Court's ruling reduced Uber drivers' incomes by 50%-60% overnight is an exaggeration and lacks substantial evidence. The impact on drivers' incomes can vary based on various factors, including the number of hours worked and the specific market conditions.

The suggestion that active black cab drivers are booking Ubers because they are cheaper and more comfortable overlooks the fact that different passengers have varying preferences and needs. It is not representative to claim that all active black cab drivers prefer Uber.

The argument that black cab drivers received non-refundable grants from the government to buy new vehicles during the pandemic while Uber was the only option for transportation in London oversimplifies the complexities of government support programs and fails to acknowledge the challenges faced by all drivers during the pandemic.

The claim that there is enough money in the market for everyone and overregulation of private hire is a hindrance to competition lacks a nuanced understanding of market dynamics and the need for regulatory measures to ensure fair and safe operations.

The allegation that the Supreme Court's ruling was influenced by political connections and lobbying efforts lacks substantial evidence and undermines the integrity of the judicial system. Courts are expected to make decisions based on legal principles and evidence presented, not political influence.

The suggestion that taxi drivers were absent during the height of the pandemic while Uber drivers served patients and medical staff overlooks the fact that the pandemic affected the entire transportation industry, including taxis. The challenges faced by all drivers during the pandemic should be viewed with empathy and understanding, rather than used to fuel division and resentment.

The claim that Uber has been highly beneficial for the economy compared to the taxi industry because a higher percentage of money on the platform goes back into the real economy lacks empirical evidence. Both the taxi industry and ride-sharing platforms contribute to the economy in various ways, and their impacts are multifaceted.

The assertion that the downfall of Uber drivers has been supported and accelerated by the taxi industry through political connections and lobbying efforts lacks substantial evidence. It is important to consider that various stakeholders, including regulatory bodies, have engaged in discussions and decision-making processes regarding the ride-sharing industry.

In conclusion, the text contains numerous unsupported claims and generalisations about the taxi industry and the Supreme Court's ruling. It is crucial to critically evaluate such claims and rely on accurate information and verified sources to form a fair and informed understanding of the issues presented.

FACT-CHECKING Point 14 of the study called:
"Uber During The Pandemic"

The text presents a distorted view of the Supreme Court ruling and makes baseless claims about Uber's actions and the government's intentions. Let's examine the claims made and provide a critical assessment:

The assertion that governments around the world deliberately took measures to reduce people's incomes during the pandemic is a conspiracy theory without any factual basis. Governments implemented various measures to mitigate the economic impact of the pandemic and support individuals and businesses.

The comparison between independent artists on different platforms, such as Fiverr and Freelancer, and taxi drivers does not provide a valid analogy. Each industry operates under different dynamics, and it is not accurate to assume that the motivations and interactions of individuals within these industries are the same.

The claim that the Supreme Court considered Uber drivers a guild and employed them is a misrepresentation of the ruling. The court's decision was based on the legal classification of drivers as workers, entitled to certain protections and benefits, not on the assumption of a guild.

The assertion that Uber did not create a PR campaign to showcase the bravery and sacrifice of their drivers during the pandemic overlooks the numerous instances where Uber acknowledged and expressed gratitude for their drivers' efforts. Uber provided support for drivers and implemented safety measures during the pandemic.

The suggestion that Uber drivers were not afraid of the virus and were the most exposed group is unfounded. The risk of exposure and the fear associated with the virus varied among individuals, and it is incorrect to assume that all Uber drivers shared the same experience or level of risk.

The claim that the government did not care about helping ill people during the pandemic, based on the lack of available public transport for doctors and nurses, is a baseless assumption. Governments faced unprecedented challenges during the pandemic and implemented various measures to ensure the provision of healthcare services.

The statement that Uber's audacity to keep more from fares contributed to the nightmare that drivers are living in nowadays lacks context. Fare structures and driver earnings are influenced by various factors, including market conditions and business decisions. It is an oversimplification to attribute drivers' current challenges solely to Uber's actions.

The suggestion that overregulation and government control over corporate operations are the new pandemic for drivers and riders is an exaggeration and mischaracterisation. Regulatory measures are implemented to ensure fair and safe operations within the transportation industry, and they are subject to ongoing discussions and revisions.

The claim that the government forced self-employed people to work through third-party companies and earn less money during the pandemic lacks evidence and appears to be a generalisation without factual basis.

The mention of the author's literary works in relation to the pandemic is unrelated and serves as a diversion from the main topic at hand.

In conclusion, the text contains unfounded conspiracy theories, misrepresentations of the Supreme Court ruling, and baseless claims about Uber's actions and the government's intentions. It is important to rely on accurate information and verified sources when discussing the impact of the pandemic and regulatory measures on the transportation industry.

FACT-CHECKING Point 15 of the study called:
"S.O.S. (The Economy)"

The text presents a series of misguided arguments and oversimplifications about the economy, the gig economy, and the role of companies like Uber. Let's examine the claims made and provide a critical assessment.

The assertion that the two most unhelpful groups for the economy are people living on benefits and the employed is an oversimplification that ignores the diverse contributions individuals from various socioeconomic backgrounds make to the economy. The economy relies on a mix of workers, entrepreneurs, and consumers, and generalising entire groups as unhelpful is misleading.

The claim that financial stability would eliminate the need for jobs and make everyone self-employed is unrealistic. While self-employment can offer certain benefits, it is not a feasible option for everyone, and the job market requires a diverse range of skills and employment opportunities.

The assertion that paying taxes is always detrimental and that corruption is inherent in a centralised authority is an extreme and unsubstantiated view. Taxes play a crucial role in funding public services, infrastructure, and social programs. While corruption exists in various forms, it does not negate the importance of taxation or the necessity of a functioning government.

The suggestion that the only solution is complete decentralisation and reliance on spontaneous councils overlooks the complexity of governance and the need for structured decision-making processes. Decentralisation alone does not guarantee effective problem-solving or societal well-being.

The claim that more independent contractors lead to greater business diversity while employed people stifle creativity is an oversimplification. Business diversity depends on various factors, including market dynamics, competition, and consumer demand. Employment status alone does not determine creativity or diversity within an industry.

The statement that Uber drivers used to make £6,000 per month in 2019 compared to significantly lower earnings today lacks context. Earnings in the gig economy can fluctuate based on multiple factors, including market conditions and individual circumstances. It is incorrect to attribute the decline in earnings solely to government actions or the implementation of Central Bank Digital Currency (CBDC).

The suggestion that accepting a CBDC would make individuals poor, compliant, and restrict their lives lacks evidence and is based on unfounded assumptions. CBDCs are still being explored by governments worldwide, and their potential impact on individuals' financial well-being is subject to ongoing discussion and analysis.

The claim that Uber drivers' earnings actively stimulate the local economy by spending their income is not exclusive to Uber drivers. All workers, regardless of their employment status, contribute to the economy through their spending habits.

The assertion that Uber paying tax on less than 25% of its income is acceptable because it followed tax laws at the time is questionable. The issue of tax avoidance and the fairness of tax obligations for companies in the gig economy are topics of ongoing debate and scrutiny.

The statement that Uber's disappearance would have a significant negative impact on the economy, leaving drivers and riders without convenient transportation options, oversimplifies the complexity of the transportation industry and alternative services available.

The suggestion that independent contractors are better for the economy than employees or people on benefits oversimplifies the relationship between employment models and their impact on overall economic well-being. It disregards the value of benefits and protections that come with employment and overlooks the potential exploitation of independent contractors.

In conclusion, the text presents a series of flawed arguments and oversimplifications regarding the economy, taxation, employment models, and the gig economy. It is important to critically evaluate these claims and consider a comprehensive understanding of economic systems and their impacts on individuals and society as a whole.

FACT-CHECKING Point 16 of the study called:
"The Silent Voices - Riders"

The text presents a series of exaggerated and unfounded claims about the current state of ride-sharing platforms, specifically focusing on Uber. Let's analyse the assertions made and provide a critical assessment.

The statement that it takes hours to book a driver on the Uber platform is an exaggeration. While there may be occasional delays due to high demand or driver availability, it is not the norm to wait for hours to secure a ride. The vast majority of Uber users can book a ride within a reasonable timeframe.

The claim that Uber is withholding more than they should and drivers are being "screwed over" lacks evidence and disregards the complex dynamics of pricing and driver compensation. Uber's business model involves balancing driver earnings with competitive pricing for riders, and driver earnings can vary based on factors such as time, distance, and surge pricing.

The suggestion that reverting to the pre-pandemic system would allow drivers to thrive and make as much money as they want overlooks the evolving regulatory landscape and the need for fair working conditions for drivers. Changes in regulations and employment classifications aim to protect drivers and ensure a more sustainable gig economy.

The statement that Uber and other platforms should never treat drivers as workers goes against the ongoing debates surrounding worker rights and protections. Treating drivers as independent contractors without any benefits or labor rights can lead to exploitation and income instability.

The assertion that most MPs are Freemasons and their solutions are not meant to make things right is a baseless conspiracy theory that lacks evidence. Accusing MPs of ulterior motives undermines the democratic process and overlooks the diverse backgrounds and motivations of elected officials.

The claim that a small minority of drivers and unions have ruined the lives of millions is an oversimplification and disregards the broader context of worker advocacy and efforts to improve labor conditions. Unions play a vital role in representing workers' interests and advocating for fair treatment.

The suggestion to bombard authorities and institutions with individual letters simultaneously is an unrealistic and impractical approach to effect change. It is essential to engage in constructive dialogue and follow established channels for communication and advocacy.

In conclusion, the text relies on exaggerated claims, conspiracy theories, and misguided assumptions about the gig economy, Uber, and the role of government and regulatory bodies. It is important to critically evaluate the assertions made and consider evidence-based arguments when discussing labor rights, worker protections, and the functioning of ride-sharing platforms.

FACT-CHECKING Point 17 of the study called:
"The Silent Voices - Drivers"

The text presents several misguided and unfounded claims about the gig economy, specifically focusing on Uber drivers.

The authors' claim that drivers are the backbone of the Uber business is exaggerated. While drivers play an essential role in the ride-sharing platform, it is crucial to recognise that Uber's success is also dependent on other factors such as technology, market demand, and user experience.

The statement that almost all rental vehicles cost about £1,000-£1,500 per month and that cheaper rental options are not viable overlooks the variety of rental plans and options available to drivers. Rental prices can vary based on location, vehicle type, and rental period, and some drivers may find renting more cost-effective than purchasing a vehicle.

The suggestion that Uber should compensate drivers more for bad riders is not practical and overlooks the complexities of rating systems and dispute resolution. Uber already has mechanisms in place to address rider behaviour issues, and it is the responsibility of drivers to report any incidents or concerns.

The assertion that drivers should never be treated as workers and should always remain independent contractors is a narrow perspective that dismisses the ongoing debates about worker rights and protections. Employment classification for gig economy workers is a complex issue, and some drivers may seek better labor protections and benefits as workers.

The claim that Uber is after drivers' data to use it in fully autonomous vehicles is speculative and lacks evidence. While Uber and other companies may collect data for various purposes, the idea that they are solely interested in using it for autonomous vehicles is nothing short of just an assumption.

The suggestion that drivers should demand a full audit from Uber overlooks the practicality of such a request and the complexity of auditing large corporations. Additionally, the claim that drivers should be compensated massively for contributing to technological advancement is not supported by any legal or contractual basis.

The assertion that joining unions is detrimental and will lead to drivers being poor and bitter is a biased and dismissive view of labor organising. Unions play an important role in advocating for workers' rights and improving labor conditions, and some drivers may find value in union representation.

The text also makes personal attacks on Freemasons and includes conspiracy theories that are not relevant to the topic of Uber drivers and the gig economy. These claims are baseless and detract from the credibility of the overall argument.

In conclusion, the text contains numerous exaggerated claims, conspiracy theories, and biased perspectives about Uber drivers and the gig economy. It is essential to critically evaluate the assertions made and rely on evidence-based arguments when discussing worker rights, labor conditions, and the functioning of ride-sharing platforms.

FACT-CHECKING Point 18 of the study called:
"The Silent Voices - MPs"

The text makes several unfounded assumptions and uses a conspiratorial tone to portray politicians and Members of Parliament (MPs) as conspirators against Uber drivers. As a fact-checking reporter, it is crucial to examine the claims critically.

The claim that politicians and MPs are facing difficulty booking Uber rides is unsubstantiated. There is no evidence provided to support this assertion, and it seems more like a baseless assumption to create a negative image of politicians.

The statement that MPs should come forward to explain the legal action against Uber lacks context and specificity. The legal actions against Uber have involved various factors, including worker classification, safety concerns, and regulatory compliance. It is not solely the responsibility of MPs to explain legal proceedings.

The assertion that the cancellation of Uber's license was a cover-up for Transport for London's (TfL) failings is a serious accusation without any evidence. TfL's decisions regarding Uber's license involve extensive reviews and considerations of various factors related to public safety and compliance.

The claim that the changes in driver status were demanded by a handful of drivers and that MPs are part of a covert operation against drivers is a conspiracy theory without any basis. Worker classification and labor issues are complex topics that involve legal, ethical, and economic considerations, and they are not driven by a few individuals or a secret plot.

The suggestion that MPs are deliberately ignoring the issues faced by Uber drivers and riders is speculative and dismissive. MPs have multiple responsibilities and agendas to address, and assuming they are intentionally neglecting an entire industry is unfair and lacks evidence.

The portrayal of Uber drivers as struggling victims and millions of riders as dependent on the service oversimplifies the situation. While some drivers may face challenges, others may find the gig economy advantageous, and riders have various transportation options beyond Uber.

In conclusion, the text relies on conspiracy theories and sensational claims to present politicians and MPs as conspirators against Uber drivers. As a fact-checking reporter, it is essential to separate fact from fiction and avoid making assumptions or endorsing baseless allegations. Examining issues related to the gig economy, worker rights, and public policy requires a more nuanced and evidence-based approach.

FACT-CHECKING Point 19 of the study called:
"The Corrupt Unions"

The text presents a highly biased and dismissive view of unions and union leaders, making unfounded accusations and promoting conspiracy theories. As a fact-checking reporter, it is essential to critically analyse the claims made and provide a more balanced perspective.

1. The claim that unions are "businesses in the true sense of the word" and live off membership fees is a misleading oversimplification. Unions are nonprofit organisations representing the interests of their members and advocating for better working conditions, wages, and benefits. While they may collect membership fees to fund their operations, equating them to profit-driven businesses is inaccurate.

2. Accusing the ADCU union founders of questionable financial sources without any evidence is a baseless allegation. Without concrete proof, such claims are mere conjecture and undermine the credibility of the argument.

3. The suggestion that the ADCU union caused harm to drivers and destroyed the business for tens of thousands of drivers is an exaggeration. The legal

actions taken by the union aimed to address worker classification and labor rights issues, which can have broader implications but are not tantamount to destruction.

4. The comparison of the union's actions to terrorism is inflammatory and lacks any basis in reality. Equating lawful legal action with terrorism is a sensational and disrespectful comparison.

5. Implying that all union leaders are members of secret societies and recommending hiring private detectives to investigate them is a far-fetched conspiracy theory. Making such claims without providing any evidence undermines the credibility of the argument.

6. The statement that any Uber driver must be their own leader is a simplistic view of the challenges faced by gig workers. Collective action through unions allows workers to amplify their voices and negotiate with companies on a more equal footing.

7. The claim that unions fail to obtain benefits greater than inflation is an oversimplification of the complex dynamics of labor negotiations. Wage increases and benefits can vary depending on various factors, including economic conditions, industry norms, and the strength of the union's bargaining power.

In conclusion, the text presents a dismissive and

conspiratorial view of unions and their leaders, relying on unfounded allegations and sensationalism to discredit their actions. As a fact-checking reporter, it is important to provide a more balanced and evidence-based analysis of labor issues and the role of unions in protecting workers' rights.

FACT-CHECKING Point 20 of the study called:
"Workers"

As a fact-checking reporter, it is important to approach the text with a critical mindset and provide a more balanced analysis of the claims made.

1. The author's derogatory language and insults towards those who seek worker protections are uncalled for and undermine the credibility of their argument. Resorting to name-calling and personal attacks does not contribute to a constructive discussion.

2. The author claims that workers' law should not protect self-employed individuals because they manage their finances better and have more freedom. However, this is an oversimplification, as many self-employed individuals face financial insecurity and lack access to benefits that workers enjoy.

3. The author's assertion that workers are seeking a comfortable and secure retirement and are not focused on creating a good life for themselves in the present is a generalisation and does not consider the diverse goals and aspirations of workers.

4. The text implies that workers who advocate for labor rights and protections are simply looking to be

slaves of the rich. This is a mischaracterisation and dismissive of the legitimate concerns of workers regarding fair treatment and compensation.

5. The text makes unfounded accusations against specific individuals and unions without providing concrete evidence to support these claims. Engaging in such character assassination without evidence undermines the credibility of the argument.

6. The notion that workers who sought to be treated as workers by companies like Uber have caused damage to self-employed drivers is an overgeneralisation. Labor rights advocacy seeks to address systemic issues and does not necessarily target self-employed individuals negatively.

7. The authors' belief that they will not benefit financially from the actions of labor rights advocates suggests a self-centered perspective, and it is not a valid justification for dismissing the legitimate concerns of workers.

In conclusion, the text employs derogatory language, personal attacks, and unfounded accusations to dismiss the importance of workers' rights and protections. As a fact-checking reporter, it is crucial to provide a more balanced and evidence-based analysis that respects the diversity of perspectives and experiences in the labor market.

FACT-CHECKING Point 21 of the study called:
"Uber's Business Costs"

As a fact-checking reporter, it's important to provide a more critical analysis of the claims made in the text.

1. The author dismisses concerns about companies like Uber not paying enough taxes, attributing it to a lack of understanding of how businesses work. However, tax avoidance and aggressive tax planning by large corporations have been well-documented issues, and these practices can indeed impact the economy by reducing the tax revenue available for public services and infrastructure.

2. The text suggests that the main problem with the economy is mishandling tax money, too many employees, and benefit claims, while advocating for more independent professionals. This oversimplifies the complexities of the economy and ignores other crucial factors that contribute to its performance, such as global economic trends, monetary policies, and fiscal management.

3. The author makes a speculative claim about Uber's business costs and tax payments without providing concrete evidence or sources to support their assertions. Without verifiable information, these claims lack credibility.

4. The text implies that those calling for more taxes from Uber are conspirators, agitators, or uneducated individuals. This is a sweeping generalisation that dismisses legitimate concerns about corporate tax responsibility and societal contributions.

5. The authors' remarks about Jewish people teaching financial education to their children are irrelevant and potentially offensive. Making generalisations based on ethnicity is not appropriate and does not contribute to a constructive discussion.

6. The text assumes that treating drivers as workers results in less tax revenue and negatively affects the economy. However, this conclusion overlooks potential benefits, such as increased worker protections, improved job stability, and reduced income inequality.

7. The text suggests that regulators intentionally colluded to harm the economy by treating drivers as workers without providing any evidence to support this serious accusation. Such claims require verifiable evidence and cannot be made based on assumptions.

8. The analogy comparing drivers being treated as workers to people in third-world countries receiving medicines instead of infrastructure improvements is not valid. These are vastly different contexts, and the comparison oversimplifies complex issues related to

labor rights and economic development.

In conclusion, the text presents a dismissive and speculative perspective on various issues, lacking concrete evidence to support its claims. As a fact-checking reporter, it is essential to avoid making sweeping generalisations and to provide well-researched, evidence-based analysis.

FACT-CHECKING Point 22 of the study called:
"Uber's Rejected Trips"

As a fact-checking reporter, I must address some questionable claims and provide a more critical analysis of the text.

1. The text asserts that there were approximately 150 million trips being rejected by drivers in a 30-day period at the end of 2022. However, there is no verifiable source or evidence provided to support this claim, making it difficult to assess its accuracy.

2. The text suggests that the expansion of the Ultra Low Emission Zone (ULEZ) zone will force many drivers to admit that being an Uber driver is no longer viable. While ULEZ may have implications for some drivers, the text makes sweeping assumptions about its impact on all Uber drivers without presenting any data or concrete evidence.

3. The text implies that switching to electric vehicles is no longer feasible for Uber drivers, but it lacks specific information about the challenges and potential solutions. Electric vehicle adoption is a complex issue that involves various factors such as infrastructure, government incentives, and technological advancements.

4. The text makes claims about the "economical situation of the individual" without providing a clear and comprehensive analysis of the broader economic context or considering other factors that could influence individual financial situations.

5. The text states that Uber is blocking riders from booking trips and keeping too much from the fare without providing credible evidence or data to support these claims. Accusations of such magnitude require verifiable sources.

6. The text suggests that politicians and corporate executives are intentionally hiding the truth and engaging in psychological manipulation without offering substantial evidence to back these claims.

7. The text acknowledges that its claims are controversial and based on "facts known only if you're a driver" without elaborating on the specific sources or experiences from which these facts are derived. This lack of transparency undermines the credibility of the claims.

In conclusion, the text contains various claims that lack verifiable evidence and fails to provide a comprehensive analysis of the issues at hand. As a fact-checking reporter, it is crucial to remain skeptical and demand solid evidence before accepting claims as facts. Providing credible sources and supporting data is essential for building a well-informed and accurate narrative.

FACT-CHECKING Point 23 of the study called:
"The Consequences Of Uber's Imminent Downfall"

As a fact-checking reporter, I must critically assess the claims made in the text and address some issues:

1. The text suggests that Uber drivers played a significant role during the COVID-19 pandemic, implying that they were instrumental in preventing the crisis from becoming much worse. While some Uber drivers may have provided essential transportation services, it is an exaggeration to claim that their actions alone prevented a deeper crisis. Multiple factors, including government policies, healthcare systems, and public cooperation, contributed to managing the pandemic's impact.

2. The text claims that Uber drivers were the "most exposed group of people in the whole of the UK" but fails to provide any verifiable data or evidence to support this assertion. Making such a sweeping statement without credible sources undermines the credibility of the claim.

3. The text portrays Uber drivers as heroes for continuing to work during the pandemic, but it neglects to mention the health and safety risks they faced while doing so. While some drivers may have

contributed positively, others might have worked due to financial constraints or lack of support, which could also have put their health at risk.

4. The text states that Uber drivers "need to earn decent and sufficient money, not barely survival money." While it's essential for workers to earn a fair wage, the text does not provide a clear definition of what constitutes "decent and sufficient money" or offer any specific solutions to address this concern.

5. The text implies that Uber's potential collapse in the UK would have catastrophic consequences for the economy and human life without providing a comprehensive analysis or evidence to support this assertion. This kind of doomsday scenario lacks a balanced consideration of other possible outcomes.

6. The text calls for "hefty compensation for years of distress caused by all these factors" without providing a well-founded justification or explanation of who should provide this compensation and how it should be implemented.

In conclusion, the text makes sweeping claims without substantial evidence, uses emotional language to appeal to readers' sentiments, and oversimplifies complex issues. As a fact-checking reporter, it is essential to critically examine all claims and demand credible evidence before accepting statements as factual. Providing concrete data, verifiable sources, and a balanced analysis is crucial for maintaining credibility and avoiding misleading narratives.

FACT-CHECKING Point 24 of the study called:
"Driver Costs Now"

The text makes several claims regarding the impact of Uber drivers' operations on the environment and their profitability. However, it lacks substantial evidence and makes sweeping generalisations. Let's address some of the issues with the text:

1. The text implies that Uber drivers are crucial for reducing congestion and promoting the "green" agenda. While some drivers may offer an alternative to private car ownership, the claim that Uber drivers significantly contribute to reducing congestion and promoting environmental sustainability lacks solid evidence. The environmental impact of ride-hailing services like Uber is complex and varies depending on several factors.

2. The text compares the costs of driving a Tesla Model 3 to a Toyota Corolla hybrid and argues that driving an electric vehicle (EV) like the Tesla is unprofitable. However, it does not provide a comprehensive analysis of all the costs involved, such as insurance, maintenance, and taxes, which can significantly impact profitability.

3. The text dismisses plug-in hybrids as the worst vehicles and accuses TfL of hypocrisy for licensing

them. While plug-in hybrids may have limitations, such as limited electric-only range, they can still provide environmental benefits when used correctly. The claim that they are less "green" than full petrol vehicles lacks nuanced consideration of their overall environmental impact.

4. The text suggests that Uber drivers are facing a "tragedy of gigantic proportions" due to various factors like increasing rider requests, decreasing driver numbers, and overregulation. However, it fails to provide verifiable data or evidence to support this claim and doesn't offer a balanced analysis of the ride-hailing industry's complexities.

5. The text portrays Tesla vehicles as the best performers among electric vehicles without providing objective data or conducting a comprehensive comparison with other electric vehicle models. This one-sided view lacks credibility and ignores the diversity of electric vehicle options available in the market.

In conclusion, the text makes grandiose claims without sufficient evidence, cherry-picks data to support its arguments, and disregards the multifaceted nature of the ride-hailing industry and environmental considerations. As a fact-checking reporter, it is crucial to demand concrete evidence and a balanced analysis of complex issues before accepting claims as valid. Without credible data, the text's arguments remain speculative and lack substantial support.

FACT-CHECKING Point 25 of the study called:
"Driver Costs Then"

The text presents speculative claims without providing concrete evidence and relies on unfounded conspiracy theories. As a fact-checking reporter, it is crucial to analyse such claims critically and seek verifiable data to determine their validity. Let's address some of the problematic points in the text.

1. The text assumes that Uber drivers had substantial income and plenty of time off in the past without providing any data or sources to support this claim. It makes assumptions about driver earnings without considering factors like expenses, taxes, and market conditions.

2. The text suggests that all policies around the world are meant to reduce the population, following a secretive global agenda. However, it provides no credible evidence or sources to back up this extraordinary claim. It is essential to approach such conspiracy theories with skepticism and demand verifiable evidence.

3. The text implies that politicians and regulators are members of secret societies, but it fails to provide any concrete proof of such affiliations. Making unsubstantiated claims about the connections of

public officials lacks credibility and can be misleading.

4. The text promotes a "global agenda 2030" theory, suggesting that governments are deliberately impoverishing Uber drivers and other workers to fit a specific narrative. Again, it lacks evidence to support this theory and overlooks the complexity of economic policies and their impact on different industries.

5. The text claims that the authors, former border police officers, have seen a lot and possess undisclosed information. However, it offers no specifics or verifiable data to validate their credibility or the legitimacy of their claims.

6. The text encourages readers to conduct in-depth research about global policies and spheres of influence, but it fails to provide specific sources or references for readers to investigate further.

As a fact-checking reporter, it is essential to be critical of such claims and demand reliable evidence before accepting them as valid. The text relies on vague assertions and unfounded conspiracy theories without providing any verifiable data or credible sources. It is crucial to separate factual information from speculative claims based on evidence-based research and verifiable data. Without concrete evidence, the claims in the text remain mere speculations and should not be taken as truth.

FACT-CHECKING Point 26 of the study called:
"Driver Sacrifices"

The text contains exaggerated and unfounded claims about Uber drivers' sacrifices, and it portrays Uber in a negative light without providing substantial evidence to support its assertions. As a fact-checking reporter, it is essential to critically analyse such claims and demand verifiable data to determine their validity. Let's address some of the problematic points in the text:

1. The text asserts that Uber drivers risked their lives during the pandemic without providing specific data or evidence to support this claim. While some drivers may have continued working during the pandemic, it is essential to avoid making generalised statements without credible sources or statistics.

2. The text accuses Uber of showing "no gratitude" to its drivers during the pandemic, implying that the company did not provide any compensation for the risks taken. This claim needs to be substantiated with concrete examples or official statements from the company to be valid.

3. The text alleges that Uber drivers have "sacrificed their finances" without providing specific data on the financial burdens they face. It is crucial to

differentiate between individual experiences and generalised claims and to consider various factors that might affect drivers' finances.

4. The text suggests that Uber drivers' sacrifices are not recognised or appreciated by the company, but it lacks concrete examples or official statements from Uber to support this assertion.

5. The text concludes by making disparaging remarks about Uber's top executives without providing any evidence or specific incidents to justify such claims. It is important to avoid making sweeping accusations without credible evidence.

6. The text implies that Uber's current business model is unsustainable and will lead to the company's failure, but it does not offer a thorough analysis or data to back up this claim. It is essential to consider multiple factors and industry trends when assessing the viability of a business model.

As a fact-checking reporter, it is crucial to avoid propagating baseless claims and seek verifiable evidence before accepting them as valid. The text contains unsubstantiated assertions and attempts to paint Uber in a negative light without providing sufficient data or credible sources. It is essential to separate factual information from speculative claims and to present a balanced view based on evidence-based research and verifiable data.

FACT-CHECKING Point 27 of the study called:
"Rider Sacrifices"

The text presents a one-sided view of the challenges faced by Uber riders and fails to consider various factors that may influence the situation. As a fact-checking reporter, it is important to critically analyse the claims made in the text and seek evidence to support or refute them. Let's address some of the issues with the text:

1. The text asserts that Uber increases fares to keep more profit under the guise of paying driver benefits without providing concrete evidence to back up this claim. While fare adjustments may occur due to various factors, it is essential to examine the reasons behind such changes and their impact on both riders and drivers.

2. The text suggests that Uber's surge pricing system charges riders more while paying drivers less per mile. However, this claim lacks specific data or official statements from Uber to support it. Surge pricing is a dynamic pricing model that may vary based on demand and supply factors, and it is important to consider its complexities before making generalisations.

3. The text claims that booking an Uber ride can be

time-consuming and frustrating without offering data
on the average booking time or comparing it to other
transportation options. It is important to consider
factors that may affect booking times, such as
demand, location, and driver availability.

4. The text implies that riders' wellbeing and lives are
at risk due to difficulties in booking Uber rides, but it
does not provide concrete examples or statistics to
support this assertion. It is crucial to differentiate
between isolated incidents and general trends to
understand the overall impact on riders' safety and
wellbeing.

5. The text calls for Uber to pay drivers a minimum of
75% of fares without providing a clear rationale or
evidence for this specific percentage. Deciding on fair
driver compensation involves considering various
factors, including operational costs, market rates, and
driver preferences.

6. The text suggests that Uber is going against its idea
of affordable and reliable transportation service, but it
does not consider the complexities and challenges
involved in providing such services at scale. It is
crucial to assess the efforts made by Uber to address
these issues and improve its services continually.

As a fact-checking reporter, it is essential to
present a balanced view and avoid making sweeping
statements without credible evidence. The text

presents a negative portrayal of Uber without thoroughly examining the underlying factors and industry dynamics. To provide a more accurate assessment, it is necessary to consider multiple perspectives and seek verifiable data from reliable sources.

FACT-CHECKING Point 28 of the study called:
"Forced Switch To Electric"

The text's claims about the challenges faced by Uber drivers in transitioning to electric vehicles lack sufficient evidence and oversimplify the complexities of the situation. As a fact-checking reporter, it is essential to critically assess the assertions made in the text and seek verifiable data to support or disprove them. Let's address the issues with the text.

1. The text claims that the mandate to switch to electric vehicles is placing a heavy financial burden on Uber drivers without providing specific data or evidence to back up this statement. The cost of electric vehicles and their financial implications for drivers may vary depending on factors such as vehicle models, available incentives, and charging infrastructure.

2. The text suggests that Uber, the government, and Transport for London are not providing sufficient financial support or incentives for drivers to switch to electric vehicles, but it lacks detailed information on the existing programs or initiatives aimed at supporting this transition.

3. The text mentions that electric vehicles have low mileage and slow charging capabilities, but it does

not provide data on the average mileage of electric vehicles used by Uber drivers or the charging infrastructure available to them.

4. The text claims that Uber drivers' income has dropped significantly due to worker status without offering concrete evidence or comparing earnings data before and after the change in employment status.

5. The text asserts that many drivers have reported a 50-60 percent drop in income without citing the sources of these reports or considering other potential factors that may have influenced their earnings.

6. The text implies that the push towards electric vehicles is noble but overlooks the potential environmental and long-term cost-saving benefits of adopting cleaner and more sustainable transportation options.

As a fact-checking reporter, it is crucial to present a balanced view and avoid making broad statements without credible evidence. The text presents a negative portrayal of the transition to electric vehicles for Uber drivers without thoroughly examining the various factors at play. To provide a more accurate assessment, it is necessary to consider multiple perspectives, seek verifiable data from reliable sources, and analyse the long-term implications of adopting electric vehicles for both drivers and the environment.

FACT-CHECKING Point 29 of the study called:
"Communication With Uber"

The claims made in the text about Uber's communication with its drivers are exaggerated and lack substantial evidence to support them. As a fact-checking reporter, it is crucial to critically assess the assertions made in the text and seek verifiable data to either confirm or debunk the claims. Here are the issues with the text.

1. The text states that Uber's communication with its drivers is lacking, but it does not provide concrete data or surveys to support this claim. It is essential to present specific examples or statistics to demonstrate the extent of the communication breakdown.

2. The text suggests that Uber uses preset scripts for responses, but it fails to provide evidence of this practice. Without verifiable sources or specific cases, it is challenging to validate this claim.

3. The text claims that Uber disregards drivers' demands, but it does not present evidence of how Uber has ignored drivers' feedback or requests.

4. The text alleges that Uber is unapproachable when it comes to explaining decisions, but it does not provide examples of instances where drivers sought

explanations and were met with unresponsiveness.

5. The text asserts that Uber's communication breakdown leads to a loss of trust and ultimately, a loss of business, but it does not offer data or market trends to support this hypothesis.

As a fact-checking reporter, it is vital to present a balanced view and avoid making sweeping statements without credible evidence. The text portrays Uber's communication with drivers in an entirely negative light without thoroughly examining the various factors at play. To provide a more accurate assessment, it is necessary to consider multiple perspectives, seek verifiable data from reliable sources, and analyse Uber's overall communication practices with drivers. Without concrete evidence, the claims made in the text remain unsubstantiated and speculative.

FACT-CHECKING Point 30 of the study called:
"What Needed To Change"

The claims made in the text regarding Uber's communication with its drivers and driver compensation are unrealistic and fail to consider the complexities of the ride-sharing industry. As a fact-checking reporter, it is essential to critically assess these assertions and provide a more balanced perspective. Here are the issues with the text.

1. The text suggests that improved communication with drivers could have been achieved simply through personalised responses and open dialogue. However, in reality, Uber's vast network of drivers makes it challenging to provide individualised responses to each driver. Moreover, open dialogue might not always be feasible due to the sheer volume of drivers and logistical constraints.

2. The text advocates for increased compensation for drivers in various situations, including waiting time, cancelled rides, and damages. While it is reasonable to consider driver compensation, it is essential to remember that ride-sharing platforms like Uber operate in a highly competitive market, where fares are often set to attract both riders and drivers. Implementing such extensive compensation measures may lead to higher costs for riders, potentially making

the service less attractive.

3. The text proposes offering better protection to drivers against bad or dangerous riders through an anti-alias system and rider screening. While safety is crucial, implementing such measures may raise privacy concerns and create challenges in verifying user identities. Moreover, rider refusal based on limited information may lead to discriminatory practices.

4. The text calls for an improved fare structure to ensure that drivers are paid more consistently. However, fare calculations in the ride-sharing industry are influenced by various factors, including distance, time, demand, and location. Guaranteeing consistent fare increases for drivers may not be financially viable for the company and could lead to unsustainable business practices.

As a fact-checking reporter, it is essential to acknowledge that the ride-sharing industry operates within a complex ecosystem of supply and demand dynamics, safety considerations, and financial constraints. While it is reasonable to consider ways to enhance communication and driver benefits, the solutions proposed in the text may not be practical or feasible. To provide a more accurate assessment, it is necessary to explore alternative approaches and consider the broader implications of any proposed changes to Uber's business model.

FACT-CHECKING Point 31 of the study called:
"What Needed No Change"

The claims made in the text regarding Uber's classification of drivers as workers and its impact on their livelihoods require a more critical analysis. As a fact-checking reporter, it is essential to question the assumptions made and consider alternative perspectives. Here are the issues with the text.

1. The text suggests that the implementation of the UK Supreme Court's decision has sparked an unnecessary controversy. However, it is crucial to recognise that the court's decision was based on legal considerations and aimed at ensuring that workers receive the rights and benefits they are entitled to under the law. The controversy arises from Uber's previous classification of drivers as independent contractors, which some argue was a misclassification to avoid providing certain benefits.

2. The text claims that many drivers argue they are not workers due to their flexibility to choose when to work and the power over the contract. While drivers may have some flexibility, this does not necessarily preclude them from being classified as workers under employment law. The court's decision took into account various factors, including the level of control Uber has over drivers' work, to determine their

employment status.

3. The text asserts that drivers should be paid at least 75% of the fares they earn to make a living wage. However, the fare structure in the ride-sharing industry is influenced by various factors, and the percentage paid to drivers may vary depending on the region and market conditions. It is essential to consider the broader economic implications of increasing driver pay and how it may impact overall service affordability for riders.

4. The text states that Uber has ignored drivers' concerns and alienated its most important asset. However, it is crucial to recognise that Uber's compliance with the court's decision is not necessarily a disregard for drivers' concerns. The company may have legal obligations and may be working to find a balance between regulatory requirements and driver demands.

As a fact-checking reporter, it is essential to recognise that the classification of drivers as workers or independent contractors is a complex legal issue with potential implications for both drivers and companies like Uber. While it is essential to consider drivers' perspectives, it is equally crucial to understand the legal context and the broader implications of any changes to the employment status of drivers. To provide a more accurate assessment, it is necessary to examine the various factors and legal considerations involved in this matter.

FACT-CHECKING Point 32 of the study called: *"The Future For Drivers"*

The claims made in the text about Uber drivers' uncertain future and the impact of worker benefits on their income require a more critical examination. As a fact-checking reporter, it is essential to question the assumptions made and consider alternative perspectives. Here are the issues with the text.

1. The text suggests that many drivers are not making a profit and are better off seeking employment elsewhere. However, it is essential to acknowledge that the gig economy, including ride-sharing platforms like Uber, is known for its flexibility and the potential for variable income. Some drivers may indeed face challenges in maintaining a consistent profit, but others may find it a viable and preferred work option due to its flexibility.

2. The text asserts that the implementation of worker benefits has had a detrimental effect on drivers' income. While it is true that providing benefits can have associated costs, it is essential to consider the broader context and the intention behind such changes. The goal of worker benefits is to ensure that drivers receive fair compensation and basic protections that are typically provided to employees in traditional employment.

3. The text claims that worker status has led to a decrease in the percentage of fares paid to drivers by Uber. However, it is important to consider the factors contributing to fare changes, such as market conditions, regulatory requirements, and company policies. The relationship between worker status and fare changes may not be as straightforward as suggested.

4. The text suggests that Uber drivers are facing increased competition from other ride-sharing services, further reducing their income. While competition in the ride-sharing industry is indeed present, it is crucial to recognise that drivers have the flexibility to choose which platforms to work for, and their income may vary based on their decisions and market conditions.

5. The text proposes that Uber needs to re-evaluate its business model and consider alternative approaches. While it is essential for companies to adapt to changing circumstances, the text does not offer specific alternative solutions or consider the potential complexities involved in implementing such changes.

As a fact-checking reporter, it is essential to recognise that the situation for Uber drivers is multi-faceted, and the challenges they face may have various contributing factors. While it is essential to consider drivers' perspectives, it is equally crucial to understand the broader context of the gig economy, regulatory requirements, and the company's business model. Providing a more accurate assessment requires a thorough examination of all relevant factors and potential solutions.

FACT-CHECKING Point 33 of the study called:
"The Future For Riders"

The claims made in the text about the uncertain future of affordable private rides for Uber riders require a more critical analysis. As a fact-checking reporter, it is essential to question the assumptions made and explore alternative viewpoints. Here are the issues with the text.

1. The text suggests that the cost of private rides is likely to increase, but it does not provide concrete evidence or data to support this claim. While it is true that costs can fluctuate in any industry, including ride-sharing, it is essential to consider various factors, such as market competition, demand, and company policies.

2. The text claims that if Uber were to fail as a business, riders may be forced to book expensive taxis. However, it ignores the possibility of other ride-sharing services or emerging competitors in the market. There are several ride-sharing platforms that may fill the void if Uber were to exit the market.

3. The text states that taxis are not subject to the same regulations as ride-sharing services, but it does not provide specific examples or evidence to support this claim. In many cities, taxis are subject to strict

regulations, including fare caps, safety requirements, and licensing.

4. The text assumes that riders would have to return to unreliable public transport if Uber were to fail, without considering the potential for improvements in public transportation or the emergence of other private transportation options.

5. The text suggests that taxis may not have the same level of convenience or ease of use as ride-sharing services, but it does not acknowledge that some riders may still prefer taxis for certain trips or circumstances.

6. The text makes a sweeping claim that some ride-sharing companies are being used for large-scale money laundering, without providing any evidence or specific examples to support this serious accusation.

As a fact-checking reporter, it is crucial to base claims on verifiable evidence and avoid making broad generalisations without adequate support. While it is important to consider the potential challenges and impacts of Uber's potential failure, it is equally essential to acknowledge the complexities of the transportation industry and the potential for other alternatives to emerge. A more comprehensive analysis is needed to assess the future of affordable private rides for Uber riders accurately.

FACT-CHECKING Point 34 of the study called:
"Net Zero Vehicles"

The claims made in the text regarding the lack of fully green vehicles and the supposed dangers of electric vehicles require a thorough fact-checking to assess their validity. As a fact-checking reporter, it is essential to examine the evidence and counterarguments to provide a comprehensive analysis.

1. Claim: There are no fully green vehicles.

Fact-Check: While it is true that no vehicle is entirely carbon-neutral or emission-free when considering the entire lifecycle, there are vehicles that significantly reduce greenhouse gas emissions and air pollutants. Electric vehicles (EVs) and hydrogen fuel cell vehicles are examples of green alternatives that have lower emissions compared to conventional gasoline or diesel-powered vehicles.

2. Claim: Electric vehicles are more dangerous to human health than classic "fossil" fuel ones.

Fact-Check: This claim is misleading and lacks scientific evidence. Electric vehicles produce zero tailpipe emissions, which means they do not release harmful pollutants like nitrogen oxides and particulate matter that can negatively impact human health. On the other hand, internal combustion engine vehicles emit harmful pollutants, contributing to air pollution and associated health issues.

3. Claim: The best and greenest vehicles at the moment are self-charging hybrids.
Fact-Check: The term "self-charging hybrid" is often used to describe hybrid vehicles that do not require external charging, relying on regenerative braking and the internal combustion engine to recharge their batteries. While these hybrids are more fuel-efficient than traditional vehicles, they still rely on gasoline, which results in emissions. Fully electric vehicles, which are charged using renewable energy sources, remain the greenest option with lower overall emissions compared to self-charging hybrids.

4. Claim: Zero emissions are not possible; it is a marketing strategy used by globalists to control minds and lives.
Fact-Check: Achieving absolute zero emissions in the transportation sector may be challenging, but significant progress has been made to reduce emissions through the adoption of electric vehicles, alternative fuels, and sustainable transportation policies. The concept of zero emissions is not a marketing strategy but a goal pursued by governments and organisations to combat climate change and reduce air pollution.

In conclusion, the claims made in the text regarding the absence of fully green vehicles, the supposed dangers of electric vehicles, and the promotion of zero emissions as a deceptive strategy lack substantial evidence. Electric vehicles, along with other sustainable transportation options, play a crucial role in reducing emissions and improving air quality. As a fact-checking reporter, it is essential to critically assess claims based on scientific evidence and objective data to provide accurate information to the public.

FACT-CHECKING Point 35 of the study called:
"Overregulation Must Stop"

The text makes some claims regarding overregulation in the private hire industry and its impact on drivers and ride-sharing companies like Uber. As a fact-checking reporter, let's critically assess these claims and provide a more balanced view.

1. Claim: Overregulation can increase costs and decrease flexibility for drivers.

Fact-Check: While some regulations may impose additional costs on drivers, they are often designed to ensure safety standards and protect consumers. For instance, obtaining licenses and permits might involve costs, but they are necessary to ensure that drivers meet certain qualifications and training requirements. Additionally, certain regulations may enhance passenger safety and overall service quality, which can be beneficial for both drivers and riders.

2. Claim: Overregulation creates barriers to entry and reduces competition.

Fact-Check: Regulation can indeed impose certain requirements on new entrants, but they are usually in place to maintain industry standards and protect consumers. Striking a balance between allowing new competitors while safeguarding passenger safety is essential. Moreover, ride-sharing companies like Uber have faced criticisms over issues like labor practices, which necessitate some level of regulation to ensure fairness and workers' rights.

3. Claim: Overregulation harms customers by limiting affordable transportation options.
Fact-Check: While excessive regulation can potentially stifle innovation and limit competition, a certain level of regulation is necessary to safeguard passenger safety and ensure service quality. Unchecked competition without appropriate standards can lead to safety and reliability concerns. The goal should be to find the right balance between regulation and fostering a competitive and affordable private hire market.

4. Claim: Overregulation is anti-climate.
Fact-Check: The link between overregulation and being "anti-climate" is not entirely accurate. Many regulations aim to promote environmentally friendly practices and reduce emissions, which align with climate goals. For instance, encouraging the use of electric vehicles and promoting sustainable transportation options are common regulatory approaches to address climate concerns.

In conclusion, while overregulation can have some adverse effects on the private hire industry and ride-sharing companies like Uber, it is essential to recognise that a certain level of regulation is necessary to ensure safety, fairness, and environmental sustainability. The key lies in striking a balance between effective regulation and fostering a competitive, innovative, and environmentally responsible private hire market. It's crucial to avoid blanket statements that dismiss regulation entirely, as it plays a crucial role in protecting both drivers and riders.

FACT-CHECKING Point 36 of the study called:
"Blocking Anti-Individual, Anti-Freedom Laws For Good"

In a society that prioritises individual freedom, it is essential to acknowledge that legislative efforts made by governments are not always inherently anti-individual or anti-freedom. In fact, laws and regulations often serve the purpose of maintaining order, protecting citizens, and ensuring the greater good of society.

Claim: Legislation that restricts freedom of speech limits the ability of people to express their opinions and ideas freely.
Fact-Check: While freedom of speech is a fundamental right, it is not an absolute freedom. Certain limitations, such as hate speech or incitement to violence, are necessary to prevent harm to individuals or communities. Balanced regulations on free speech aim to protect individuals from harmful content and foster an environment of respectful discourse.

Claim: Legislation that restricts freedom of assembly limits the ability of people to gather and organise for social or political purposes.
Fact-Check: The right to assembly is indeed crucial in a democratic society, but there are instances where

restrictions on gatherings are necessary to maintain public safety, prevent violence, or ensure smooth functioning during emergencies. Governments often balance the right to assembly with the need for public order.

Claim: Legislation that is anti-individual and anti-freedom harms economic growth and development.
Fact-Check: Legislation aimed at protecting consumer rights, ensuring fair competition, and promoting responsible business practices can actually contribute to economic growth and development. Sensible regulations prevent monopolies, encourage innovation, and foster a healthy business environment.

In conclusion, while individual freedom is a cornerstone of a democratic society, labelling all legislative efforts as inherently anti-individual and anti-freedom oversimplifies the complexities of governance. It is crucial to strike a balance between personal freedoms and societal interests. Responsible regulations can enhance individual liberties, protect citizens, and foster economic growth. Rather than blocking all legislation, engaging in informed debates and advocating for well-balanced regulations is a more effective way to ensure a thriving society.

FACT-CHECKING Point 37 of the study called:
"Private Rides Are Greener Than Public Transport"

In today's world, there is an unwarranted obsession with environmental sustainability, and some people mistakenly believe that public transportation is the holy grail of eco-friendliness. However, the reality is that private hire industry and private rides can often be a more sensible and environmentally responsible choice.

Claim: Public transport systems are not always efficient, wasting valuable resources like fuel and energy.
Fact-Check: While public transport systems may not always be perfectly efficient, they are generally designed to accommodate a higher number of passengers, which can significantly reduce the carbon footprint per person compared to individual private rides. Modern public transport systems are continually improving their efficiency and adopting cleaner technologies.

Claim: Private hire industry and private rides allow for more efficient use of resources through ride-sharing and the use of hybrid or electric vehicles.
FactCheck: While ride-sharing can reduce the number

of cars on the road, it does not necessarily mean that private rides are more eco-friendly. The overall environmental impact depends on the number of passengers in each private ride and the type of vehicles used. Many cities are investing in electric buses and upgrading their public transport fleets to reduce emissions.

Claim: Private hire industry and private rides offer greater flexibility and convenience compared to public transport.

Fact-Check: Flexibility and convenience are subjective preferences, but it is crucial to consider the larger picture. Public transport systems are designed to serve a broader population efficiently, leading to overall reductions in traffic congestion and emissions compared to private rides.

In conclusion, advocating for private hire industry and private rides as a universally superior choice for the environment is misguided and factually incorrect. Public transportation remains a crucial component of sustainable urban planning and can significantly reduce the environmental impact of transportation. By investing in cleaner public transport options, encouraging ride-sharing in public transit, and promoting eco-friendly technologies, we can make substantial progress in achieving true environmental sustainability. It is essential to prioritise data-backed decisions over unfounded claims to make a real impact on our carbon footprint.

FACT-CHECKING Point 38 of the study called:
"What You Can Do As Rider"

The author's call for individual action to support Uber drivers and protect the service is misguided and lacks a clear understanding of how to address the issues at hand. Encouraging individual actions without proper coordination and leadership is nothing more than a recipe for chaos and ineffectiveness.

Claim: If drivers are suffering, the service will collapse, so riders must support the drivers' interests.

Fact-Check: While it is true that drivers are essential to the functioning of Uber, solely focusing on their interests without considering the larger picture is short-sighted. The success of Uber relies on a delicate balance between the interests of drivers, riders, and the company itself. Ignoring the sustainability of the business model is not a viable long-term solution.

Claim: Organise a legal siege aimed at various entities, including TfL, Uber, the Supreme Court, MPs, and Councils.

Fact-Check: Organising a legal siege without a clear legal basis or strategy is counterproductive. Such actions may lead to unnecessary confrontations and lack the necessary focus to effect meaningful change. The legal system operates through due process and not through individual sieges.

Claim: Do not support union action or organize protests.
Fact-Check: While individual actions can have limited impact, dismissing the power of collective action through unions and protests is dismissive of the rights of workers to organise and express their grievances. Collective action can bring attention to critical issues and influence change when done responsibly and within legal frameworks.

Claim: The government is corrupt and destabilising for its anti-freedom, anti-individual "green" agenda.
Fact-Check: Accusing the government of being corrupt and pushing an anti-freedom agenda without specific evidence is an unfounded claim. Environmental sustainability and green initiatives are essential for the well-being of our planet, and dismissing them as anti-individual is misleading and counterproductive.

In conclusion, advocating for individual actions without proper coordination and dismissing the role of unions and protests is not an effective approach to address the concerns of Uber drivers or protect the service. Meaningful change requires a balanced understanding of the complexities involved and the collaborative efforts of all stakeholders, including drivers, riders, Uber, and regulatory authorities. It is essential to support actions that are lawful, well organised, and factually grounded to achieve positive change.

FACT-CHECKING Point 39 of the study called:
"What You Can Do As Driver"

The author's approach to addressing the concerns of Uber drivers is overly simplistic and dismissive of the complexities involved. Advocating for individual legal actions without considering the broader context and legal implications is unrealistic and may lead to counterproductive outcomes.

Claim: Educate yourself. It's free! Use this book to plan your action.
Fact-Check: While self-education is essential, implying that reading a single book can provide all the necessary knowledge to plan legal actions is misleading. Legal matters are often intricate and require in-depth understanding, which cannot be achieved through one book alone.

Claim: Scale up your legal action, starting with the smallest and closest player in the game.
Fact-Check: Scaling up legal actions without proper legal representation and strategic planning can lead to legal setbacks and financial burden for individual drivers. It is essential to seek professional legal advice to understand the appropriate steps and identify the most effective course of action.

Claim: Ask for professional legal advice, but be

careful with lawyers.
Fact-Check: While seeking legal advice is crucial, painting lawyers as untrustworthy and discouraging drivers from seeking professional assistance is misleading. Lawyers are trained professionals who can provide valuable guidance and representation in legal matters.

Claim: 5,000 drivers need to engage in legal actions to overcome the ADCU.
Fact-Check: Assigning an arbitrary number of drivers needed for legal actions without considering the individual merits of each case is not based on factual evidence. Legal actions should be based on the strength of the arguments and evidence presented, not on reaching a specific number of participants.

Claim: Uber may fold its operations in the UK by 2025.
Fact-Check: Predicting the future actions of a company like Uber without solid evidence is speculative and misleading. Uber's decisions are influenced by a wide range of factors, and predicting their actions with certainty is not feasible.

In conclusion, advocating for individual legal actions without proper legal counsel and dismissing the role of collective efforts like ADCU is not a reliable strategy to address the concerns of Uber drivers. Legal matters require a comprehensive understanding of the law and a well-coordinated approach. Encouraging drivers to take on legal actions individually without considering the risks and complexities is unrealistic and may lead to unfavourable outcomes. Collaborative efforts, professional legal advice, and evidence-based actions are essential for any meaningful change in this context.

FACT-CHECKING Point 40 of the study called:
"Why You Should Do Something"

The author's claims are exaggerated and misleading, presenting a one-sided view of the situation without considering the complexities of the issues at hand. It is essential to critically analyse the arguments presented and provide a more nuanced perspective.

Claim: General conspiracy is taking us back to very dark ages, to deindustrialization, and technological regress.
Fact-Check: The notion of a "general conspiracy" taking society back to dark ages and technological regress is a baseless and unfounded claim. There is no credible evidence to support such a broad and speculative assertion.

Claim: Uber brought safety, affordability, and peace of mind to drivers and riders.
Fact-Check: While Uber has provided a convenient transportation option for many, it is misleading to suggest that it single-handedly brought safety, affordability, and peace of mind. The safety of Uber rides has been a subject of controversy, and affordability varies depending on factors like surge pricing and location.

Claim: Drivers could earn decent money, enabling

them to start other ventures and live healthy lives.
Fact-Check: The income of Uber drivers varies significantly depending on location, demand, and other factors. Presenting a blanket statement about all drivers earning decent money is not accurate. Many drivers struggle to earn a sustainable income due to various challenges within the gig economy.

Claim: Riders complaining about surge prices do not understand basic economics.
Fact-Check: Suggesting that riders who complain about surge pricing lack basic economic understanding is dismissive and overlooks legitimate concerns about price fluctuations and transparency in fare calculations.

Claim: People never complained publicly about taxi drivers charging extortionate amounts, but only about Uber.
Fact-Check: Complaints about taxi fares and services have existed long before Uber's emergence. It is incorrect to claim that people only complained about Uber and not taxis. Both ride-hailing services and traditional taxis have faced criticism from customers.

Claim: Transportation cannot be affordable at any time of day and in any conditions.
Fact-Check: While it is true that transportation costs can fluctuate based on demand, supply, and other factors, implying that transportation can never be affordable at any time is an oversimplification. Many

transportation systems aim to strike a balance between convenience and affordability for users.

In conclusion, the author's arguments lack factual evidence and are presented in a dismissive and one-sided manner. The issues surrounding ride-hailing services like Uber are complex and deserve careful analysis and consideration of different perspectives. Making broad claims without supporting evidence can mislead readers and undermine a constructive discussion of the challenges and benefits associated with such services.

FACT-CHECKING Point 41 of the study called:
"If You Don't Do Anything"

The authors' alarmist and exaggerated tone detracts from a factual and balanced analysis of the situation. It is essential to approach the claims made with a critical eye and provide a more grounded perspective.

Claim: All drivers partnered with Uber will shift to normal jobs or doing something else, and losing private hire will have deeper implications than a simple mind can comprehend.
Fact-Check: It is unlikely that all Uber drivers will immediately shift to traditional jobs or other ventures. While some drivers may transition to different employment, many factors influence their decisions, including job availability, personal circumstances, and preferences. The notion that losing private hire will have incomprehensible implications lacks concrete evidence and appears to be fear-mongering.

Claim: The importance of private hire was put to test during the 2020 pandemic and needs to thrive.
Fact-Check: While private hire services, including Uber, played a role during the pandemic, suggesting that their survival is critical based on that singular event is an exaggeration. The pandemic brought challenges to many industries, and the recovery and adaptation of transportation services should be

evaluated pragmatically.

Claim: There has never been a lower morale of Uber drivers since the start of the business in the UK.
Fact-Check: Claiming that there has never been lower driver morale is an overly dramatic statement with no substantiated evidence. Driver morale can vary based on numerous factors, including earnings, working conditions, and communication with the platform.

Claim: If this continues, many drivers will get sick if they don't move on or take action.
Fact-Check: The link between driver morale and physical health is not directly supported by evidence. While job satisfaction can impact overall well-being, stating that many drivers will get sick without providing any data is speculative and misleading.

Claim: Riders will lose affordable and instantly available private transportation, leading to negative impacts on life.
Fact-Check: While some riders may face challenges if private hire services decline, it is an exaggeration to suggest that this will lead to universally negative impacts on life. Alternative transportation options and evolving technologies may fill any gaps.

Claim: The implications of losing Uber may cause death to a lot of people.
Fact-Check: Suggesting that the loss of Uber could

lead to many deaths is a baseless and fear-based claim. There is no evidence to support such an extreme consequence.

In conclusion, the authors' claims are alarmist, speculative, and lack factual evidence. It is important to approach discussions about the future of ride-hailing services with a more balanced and evidence-based perspective, considering both the benefits and challenges associated with such platforms. Over-exaggerating the potential consequences only serves to spread fear and misinformation.

FACT-CHECKING Point 42 of the study called:
"The Big Audit"

The author's claims appear to be based on personal grievances and assumptions rather than concrete evidence. Let's fact-check and provide a more balanced perspective.

Claim: Drivers must ask Uber for a full audit to prove that the company has screwed drivers when it comes to pay.

Fact-Check: While drivers have the right to seek clarification on their pay and request an audit if they believe there are discrepancies, the author's assertion that Uber intentionally mistreated drivers is speculative. Without concrete evidence to support these claims, it's essential to approach such accusations with skepticism.

Claim: Uber was withholding money, including tips, from drivers, and there were discrepancies in the payment shown in the app and the actual amount paid.

Fact-Check: The claim that Uber was intentionally withholding money from drivers, including tips, needs to be substantiated with evidence. It is essential to consider other factors, such as payment processing and delays, before jumping to conclusions.

Claim: Drivers have power over the services contract and can demand full transparency from Uber.

Fact-Check: While drivers play a crucial role in providing services, it is essential to acknowledge that they are independent contractors, and their relationship with Uber is governed by a services contract. Demanding full transparency may not be feasible, as certain contractual terms and agreements may limit the level of information shared.

Claim: Uber is a Big Data company recording accurate details about everything drivers do on the app.

Fact-Check: While Uber collects data to enhance its services, the claim that they record "everything" drivers do may be an exaggeration. Data collection is typically carried out to improve user experiences and optimise the platform.

Claim: Uber will try to fight having audits for every driver, but drivers will have the company in the palm of their hand if they manage to get it.

Fact-Check: Suggesting that an audit will give drivers complete control over Uber's actions is a stretch. Audits are a standard business practice and do not automatically guarantee favourable outcomes for drivers.

Claim: There are 100% chances that Uber paid drivers less than they should have, leading to

severe breaches and hefty compensation.
Fact-Check: Making blanket statements like "100% chances" without specific evidence undermines the credibility of the claim. Compensation for drivers, if warranted, would depend on individual circumstances and evidence of wrongdoing.

Claim: Uber cannot win against thousands of individual legal actions.
Fact-Check: The outcome of legal actions is uncertain and depends on the strength of the evidence presented by both parties. Assuming that Uber cannot win against individual legal actions is premature and speculative.

In conclusion, while drivers have the right to seek clarity on their earnings and request audits if necessary, it is crucial to substantiate claims with evidence rather than speculative assumptions. Calling for audits and seeking transparency is reasonable, but making sweeping accusations without concrete proof undermines the validity of the argument.

FACT-CHECKING Point 43 of the study called:
"How Uber Planned To Cause Harm To Its Drivers With Clear Intent"

The author's claims appear to be based on unsubstantiated conspiracy theories and misinformation, rather than credible evidence. Let's fact-check and provide a more rational perspective.

Claim: Uber organised a Q&A session in 2021 to promote unapproved mRNA injections to drivers across the UK, despite no casualties among Uber drivers due to COVID-19.

Fact-Check: There is no evidence to support the claim that Uber organised a Q&A session to promote unapproved mRNA injections. The information provided lacks verifiable sources, and there is no indication of any such session taking place.

Claim: The percentage of Uber drivers who passed away due to COVID-19 is zero, suggesting that COVID-19 risks were exaggerated.

Fact-Check: Without verifiable data, it is impossible to make such claims about COVID-19-related deaths among Uber drivers. The COVID-19 pandemic has affected individuals from various professions, and the absence of deaths among Uber drivers does not imply that the risks are exaggerated.

Claim: All riders who took the injections are feeling very ill, and Uber's intention was to harm drivers.

Fact-Check: Correlation does not imply causation. Linking rider experiences to vaccine injections without concrete evidence is not valid. Vaccine efficacy and safety are rigorously evaluated through clinical trials and regulatory approvals, and there is no credible evidence to suggest that Uber intends to harm drivers.

Claim: The medical professionals involved in the Q&A session are "questionable professionals" and should be banned from practicing medicine.

Fact-Check: Making sweeping judgments about medical professionals without sufficient evidence is unfair and unprofessional. It is essential to assess their qualifications, expertise, and adherence to medical standards based on credible sources.

Claim: mRNA vaccines cannot provide long-lasting immunity, and the medical professionals in the session gave incorrect information.

Fact-Check: mRNA vaccines have been shown to provide strong immunity against COVID-19, and their efficacy is supported by extensive clinical trials and real-world data. Suggesting that medical professionals provided incorrect information without credible evidence is not a valid argument.

Claim: Uber targeted racial profiles of drivers during the session to influence them to take the injections.

Fact-Check: Accusing Uber of targeting specific racial profiles without evidence is a serious claim that requires substantial proof to be taken seriously. Without verifiable data on Uber's targeting strategy, this claim remains speculative.

In conclusion, the text contains a series of baseless claims and conspiracy theories without credible evidence. It is essential to rely on factual information from reputable sources to make informed decisions regarding health and safety matters. Without proper evidence, dismissing medical professionals and promoting conspiracy theories can be misleading and harmful.

I must reiterate that the statements made in this text are not grounded in scientific evidence and promote conspiracy theories. It is essential to rely on credible sources and scientific research when discussing health-related topics, including vaccines and viruses.

Claim: The text criticises the responses of medical professionals during the Q&A session and questions their expertise.

FactCheck: The text makes bold and unsupported claims about the expertise and qualifications of the medical professionals involved in the Q&A session. It is essential to recognise that any professionals that might have been involved have undergone rigorous training and education to practice medicine, and their advice is based on scientific evidence and medical knowledge.

Claim: The mRNA vaccines are dangerous and should be avoided.

Fact-Check: mRNA vaccines, such as the ones developed for COVID-19, have undergone extensive clinical trials and regulatory approvals to ensure their safety and efficacy. They have been shown to be highly effective in preventing severe illness and death from COVID-19. Millions of people worldwide have received these vaccines without any significant safety concerns.

Claim: Immunocompromised people should not receive vaccines.

Fact-Check: Immunocompromised individuals may have reduced immune responses to vaccines, but that does not mean they should not receive them. Vaccination is especially crucial for these individuals to provide some level of protection against the disease. They may require additional medical guidance or booster doses to optimise their immune response.

Claim: The virus mutation and variants are not a cause for concern, and vaccination is unnecessary.

Fact-Check: Virus mutations are natural occurrences,

and new variants can arise over time. Some variants may have increased transmissibility or resistance to immunity, making them more concerning. Vaccination remains a crucial tool in controlling the spread of the virus, preventing severe disease, and protecting vulnerable populations.

In conclusion, the text contains numerous unfounded claims and misrepresentations about vaccines, viruses, and medical professionals. It is essential to base discussions on factual information from reputable sources and to rely on the guidance of healthcare experts and scientific research. Vaccines have played a critical role in controlling and managing infectious diseases throughout history, and they continue to be an essential tool in the fight against COVID-19. It is crucial to trust in the rigorous testing and evaluation processes that vaccines undergo to ensure their safety and effectiveness.

I must emphasise that the statements made in the text are not based on credible sources or scientific evidence. The assertions made about the mRNA technology, vaccines, and the expertise of medical professionals are unfounded and promote conspiracy theories.

Claim: The mRNA vaccines are dangerous and can lead to severe side effects, including organ damage.
Fact-Check: The mRNA vaccines, such as the ones

developed for COVID-19, have undergone extensive clinical trials involving tens of thousands of participants. These trials have shown that the vaccines are safe and effective in preventing severe illness and death from COVID-19. While some individuals may experience mild side effects after vaccination, severe side effects are rare and are closely monitored by regulatory agencies.

Claim: mRNA technology has not been thoroughly researched and is toxic for humans.

Fact-Check: mRNA technology has been researched for several decades, and the development of mRNA vaccines builds upon this extensive scientific knowledge. The technology has been studied in various contexts and has shown promise in vaccine development. The mRNA vaccines for COVID-19 have undergone rigorous testing to ensure their safety and efficacy before receiving regulatory approval for emergency use.

Claim: mRNA vaccines do not provide immunity to COVID-19.

Fact-Check: mRNA vaccines have been shown to be highly effective in preventing COVID-19 infection and reducing the severity of the disease. While breakthrough infections can occur, vaccinated individuals are much less likely to experience severe illness or hospitalisation compared to unvaccinated individuals.

In conclusion, it is crucial to rely on credible sources and scientific research when discussing health-related topics, including vaccines and viruses. The mRNA vaccines for COVID-19 have undergone thorough testing and regulatory approval to ensure their safety and effectiveness. Vaccination remains a critical tool in controlling and managing infectious diseases and protecting public health. Promoting conspiracy theories and misinformation can have serious consequences and undermine public trust in the healthcare system.

As a journalistic fact-checker, I must clarify that the conclusions drawn in the text are not based on factual information and are not supported by scientific evidence. The text contains several inaccuracies, misunderstandings, and false claims. Let's address each conclusion:

1. The conclusion states that nothing is safe and that GPs have no knowledge about vaccines and immunology. This is incorrect. Vaccines undergo rigorous testing and evaluation before being approved for use, and medical professionals, including GPs, are well-trained in vaccine science and immunology.

2. The conclusion claims that all COVID-19 vaccines contain particles that enter cells and wipe out millions of cells over time. This is not true. COVID-19 vaccines, including mRNA vaccines, do not contain live virus particles and do not cause long-term harm

to cells.

3. The conclusion states that all mRNA vaccines have caused serious side effects in 100% of cases, which is not supported by any evidence. COVID-19 vaccines, including mRNA vaccines, have undergone extensive clinical trials and real-world studies showing their safety and efficacy.

4. The conclusion suggests that medical professionals are hiding the true risks of vaccines and promoting a narrative dictated by Big Pharma. This is a baseless conspiracy theory and is not supported by any credible evidence.

5. The conclusion incorrectly asserts that taking an mRNA vaccine will give individuals more blood clots and harm their health. COVID-19 vaccines, including mRNA vaccines, have been extensively studied, and the benefits of vaccination far outweigh the risks, especially considering the risks associated with COVID-19 infection itself.

6. The conclusion claims that mRNA vaccines are not fully approved or licensed, which is untrue. As of my last knowledge update in September 2021, several mRNA vaccines, including the Pfizer-BioNTech and Moderna vaccines, have received full approval from regulatory agencies, such as the FDA in the United States.

7. The conclusion states that long COVID is not a real condition and that it is a result of misdiagnosis or lack of medical attention. Long COVID is a recognised condition characterised by persistent symptoms that can last for weeks or months after the acute phase of COVID-19 infection.

8. The conclusion dismisses the importance of testing when traveling abroad and suggests that asymptomatic individuals cannot spread the virus. COVID-19 testing is an essential tool for controlling the spread of the virus and identifying asymptomatic carriers who can transmit the virus to others.

It is important to rely on evidence-based information and consult reputable sources, such as public health authorities and medical professionals, when making decisions about vaccines and health. The text provided contains numerous inaccuracies and should not be considered reliable information.

Again, as a journalistic fact-checker, I must clarify that the text provided contains numerous inaccuracies and misinformation regarding mRNA technology, COVID-19, and vaccines. Let's address a few other key points:

1. mRNA technology and its history: The claim that mRNA technology was considered highly dangerous pre-2020 and that Moderna gave up on mRNA research due to long-term negative effects on humans

is entirely false. mRNA technology has been studied and researched for decades, starting in the 1960s, and it has shown promising potential for vaccines and therapeutics. Moderna was not involved in mRNA research back in 1986, and there is no credible evidence to support such a claim.

2. Safety of mRNA vaccines: The statement that all scientific papers on mRNA trials are horrifying to read and that safety data have been massively manipulated and fabricated is untrue. mRNA vaccines, including those for COVID-19, have undergone rigorous clinical trials, and data from these trials have been thoroughly reviewed by regulatory agencies worldwide before granting emergency use or full approvals. These vaccines have demonstrated a high safety profile in millions of people who have received them.

3. Immunity after COVID-19 infection: Contrary to the claim that immunity cannot be boosted, vaccination after recovering from COVID-19 can provide additional protection. While natural infection does provide some immunity, the level and duration of protection can vary among individuals. Vaccination ensures a more consistent and stronger immune response, leading to higher levels of protection against the virus and its variants.

4. Safety of COVID-19 vaccines and autoimmunity: The assertion that mRNA vaccines cause autoimmune

diseases like AIDS is unfounded and lacks scientific evidence. COVID-19 vaccines have not been shown to cause AIDS or similar autoimmune conditions. The mRNA vaccines authorised for emergency use or approved have undergone extensive testing and have not been associated with such severe side effects.

5. Cost of mRNA vaccines: The claim that mRNA technology is more costly compared to RNA technology is misleading. While mRNA vaccines may be more expensive to produce initially, they offer several advantages, such as rapid development and adaptability to new variants, making them highly valuable in pandemic situations.

6. Uber's role in promoting vaccines: There is no evidence to support the claim that Uber paid untrustworthy professionals to promote vaccines or that Uber has harmed its drivers by advocating vaccination. Public health authorities, scientific experts, and healthcare professionals worldwide have recommended vaccination as a crucial tool to combat the COVID-19 pandemic.

7. Zolgensma and Remdesivir: Comparing mRNA vaccines to unrelated medical treatments like Zolgensma and Remdesivir is not scientifically relevant. Zolgensma is a gene therapy used to treat spinal muscular atrophy, while Remdesivir is an antiviral medication used to treat certain viral infections. These treatments have different

mechanisms of action and purposes from mRNA vaccines.

8. Vaccination and immunity: Contrary to the claim that immunity can never be boosted, vaccines are specifically designed to stimulate the immune system to develop immunity against specific diseases. Vaccination has been a crucial tool in preventing infectious diseases and saving lives for centuries.

In conclusion, the text contains numerous false claims and misleading information about mRNA technology, vaccines, and COVID-19. It is essential to rely on credible sources, such as health authorities and scientific studies, to make informed decisions about health and vaccination. Misinformation can be harmful and may deter individuals from seeking life-saving medical interventions.

FACT-CHECKING Point 44 of the study called: *"Could Uber Stock Plunge To Under $1 Soon?"*

As a fact-checking reporter, I must point out that the text provided contains several misleading statements and speculative claims about Uber's stock and business. Let's address the key points:

1. Uber's stock price manipulation: The text suggests that Uber's stock price is being manipulated by Wall Street mechanisms and lies, and big investors are constantly pumping and dumping the stock. However, these claims lack credible evidence and fail to acknowledge the complex factors that influence stock prices, such as market sentiment, company performance, and broader economic trends.

2. "Green" agenda and downfall of Uber: The text speculates that Uber's downfall will be due to the "green" agenda being pushed onto drivers. While it is true that the company has faced challenges related to regulations and sustainability efforts, it is not accurate to attribute Uber's potential downfall solely to this factor. Business performance, competition, and market dynamics play a significant role in determining a company's success or failure.

3. Switch to autonomous vehicles: The text predicts

that the switch to fully autonomous vehicles will lead to the total collapse of Uber. While the transition to autonomous vehicles presents challenges and uncertainties, it is also seen as a potential opportunity for ride-share companies to improve efficiency and reduce costs. It is premature to claim that Uber will collapse due to autonomous vehicles, as the technology and regulatory landscape are still evolving.

4. Revenue and profitability: The text suggests that Uber does not have money for promised technological advancements and that the CEO's announcement of huge profits after the pandemic will be short-lived. These claims are speculative and lack concrete evidence to support them. Uber's financial performance and investments should be assessed based on official financial reports and disclosures.

5. Driver exodus and ridership decline: While it is true that the ride-share industry has faced challenges during the pandemic, such as a decline in ridership and driver availability, the text's assertions about the impending driver exodus and the majority of riders believing Uber is finished are unsupported and overly pessimistic.

6. Autonomous vehicles and safety concerns: The text claims that bringing in autonomous vehicles is not viable due to safety concerns, regulatory restrictions, and government resistance. While there are legitimate

safety and regulatory concerns related to autonomous vehicles, major technology and automotive companies are actively developing and testing autonomous technologies with the aim of eventually deploying them on a commercial scale.

7. Uber's future prospects: The text paints a highly negative outlook for Uber's future, projecting potential stock price crashes and the company's inability to compete in the market. It is important to consider multiple perspectives and expert analyses before making definitive claims about a company's future performance.

In conclusion, the text provided contains speculative and unsupported claims about Uber's stock and business prospects. While it is reasonable to discuss challenges and risks faced by any company, it is essential to rely on credible sources and data-backed analyses to form a well-informed view.

FACT-CHECKING the chapter called:
"The Action"

As a fact-checking reporter, I must emphasise that the text provided contains several claims and suggestions that lack solid evidence and may not accurately represent the legal situation regarding Uber drivers and their employment status. Let's address the key points and clarify some misconceptions:

1. Independent Contractors vs. Workers: The text asserts that Uber drivers should not join unions because they are independent contractors or self-employed, not workers. However, the employment status of Uber drivers has been a subject of legal dispute in various jurisdictions, and courts have ruled differently in different cases. The classification of drivers as workers or independent contractors depends on specific legal criteria and interpretations, which may vary by country or region.

2. Shaping the document for the UK Supreme Court: The text advises individuals to shape the document based on their personal situation and circumstances and send it individually. While individuals have the right to present their case, it is essential to ensure that the arguments and claims are legally sound and supported by evidence. The UK Supreme Court requires proper legal arguments and not just personal

narratives.

3. Contacting Transport for London (TfL): The text suggests contacting TfL to change licensing conditions and stop Uber from charging drivers' riders more than 25% of the fare. These demands may not be solely within the authority of TfL, as regulatory decisions involving fare percentages and business models often require careful consideration and consultation.

4. Misrepresentation by ADCU union: The text implies that the ADCU union misled the courts by presenting itself as representing all drivers without their permission and opinion. It is crucial to verify the accuracy of such claims and recognise that unions may advocate for collective interests on behalf of their members.

5. Petition and appeal process: The text mentions signing a petition and seeking permission to appeal the court's decision at a cost of £800-£1,000. While petitions can be a form of expression, they do not have a direct legal impact on court decisions. The appeal process involves legal procedures and requirements that individuals must carefully follow.

6. Contacting individual judges: The text suggests sending a shorter version of the letter to each individual judge who reasoned on the decision. However, legal communications should typically go

through the appropriate court channels and not directly to individual judges.

In conclusion, while individuals have the right to express their concerns and present their cases to the appropriate legal bodies, it is essential to base these communications on accurate legal information and sound arguments. Legal proceedings require adherence to formal procedures, and it is crucial to seek professional legal advice when navigating such matters.

FACT-CHECKING the document called:
"Skeleton Arguments for the rescinding or amending (to apply only to the Respondents) of the UK's Supreme Court Decision through its Employment Appeal Tribunal (EAT) in the final Appeal stage of the case Uber BV and others (Appellants) vs Aslam and others (Respondents)"

As a fact-checking reporter, I must point out that the text provided contains several unsubstantiated claims and assumptions that are not supported by concrete evidence. It is essential to separate opinions from verifiable facts. Let's address the key points and clarify some misconceptions:

1. Misrepresentation of the case: The text claims that the case brought by Aslam and others to the Supreme Court contained erroneous and bogus details and that the subject of the case was fabricated. However, without concrete evidence to support this claim, it remains a baseless allegation.

2. Allegations against the Plaintiff and unions: The text makes several negative assertions against the Plaintiff, Mr. Aslam, and the ADCU union, suggesting that they misled the court and manipulated drivers. Without factual evidence to support these claims, they are mere opinions and lack credibility.

3. Impact on income: The text states that drivers are making less money after the Supreme Court ruling, but it fails to provide verifiable data to support this claim. Income fluctuations can be influenced by various factors, including market conditions, demand, and platform policies.

4. Contractual changes with Uber: The text criticises Uber for changing its business model and contends that drivers should retain full control over contracts with riders. However, such contractual arrangements are subject to the terms and conditions set by Uber, and the company may have valid reasons for implementing changes to ensure compliance with legal requirements.

5. Assumptions about drivers' motivations: The text assumes that drivers who joined the legal action were either paid to do so or manipulated into participating. These are speculative assumptions without any evidence to back them up.

6. Alleged agenda behind the lawsuit: The text suggests that there is a hidden agenda to cripple

private hire drivers, but it provides no evidence to support such a claim. Legal cases are typically driven by legitimate concerns and not ulterior motives.

In conclusion, while individuals have the right to express their opinions and concerns, it is crucial to differentiate between opinions and verifiable facts. Legal matters require evidence and sound arguments, not baseless allegations or assumptions. As a fact-checking reporter, I must stress the importance of relying on credible sources and factual information when making claims or forming opinions.

Oh, give me a break! This emotional tirade from an Uber driver is nothing more than a sob story meant to paint themselves as a victim. Let's get real and start debunking these exaggerated claims.

First of all, the author tries to portray Uber drivers as some sort of pandemic heroes, claiming they were driving patients, nurses, and doctors to hospitals, putting their lives in severe danger. Please spare me the melodrama. Uber drivers were providing a service, sure, but they were also just doing their jobs like many other essential workers. Trying to make them out to be superheroes is a bit much.

And let's not forget the conspiracy theories about collusion between TfL, the taxi industry, unions, and Uber. Seriously? The author is suggesting that all these parties came together to intentionally harm private hire drivers? That's a wild and baseless accusation without any evidence to support it.

Next up, the author complains about being treated as a worker by Uber following the court's ruling. Well, newsflash, that's the whole point of the ruling! If you're acting like an employee, then you should be classified as one. It's not rocket science. The author's insistence on remaining self-employed while enjoying worker benefits is just plain greedy.

Oh, and let's not forget the rant about pension funds crashing and being unable to trust anyone with their money. Give me a break! We all have to plan for retirement, and crying about not wanting to contribute to a pension fund is just irresponsible.

As for the claim that Uber is limiting their earnings and favouring drivers who accept all trips, that's just the nature of the business. If you're choosy about which trips you take, you can't expect to make as much money as those who are more willing to work. It's called supply and demand, and it's how the real world works.

The author's complaint about not being able to know how much Uber charges riders is laughable. Why should they be privy to that information? They're providing a service, not running the platform.

Lastly, the authors' assertion that the private

hire sector is now detrimental to their health, wellbeing, and the economy is pure hyperbole. The private hire sector is just one piece of the larger economy, and it's not as crucial as the author wants to believe.

In conclusion, this text is nothing more than a self-serving and exaggerated sob story. The author needs to stop playing the victim and take responsibility for their own choices and actions. And as for the unfounded conspiracy theories, they should leave those to the realm of fiction where they belong.

The text provided appears to be an opinionated letter from a private hire driver expressing their grievances against Uber and their dissatisfaction with being classified as a worker. As a fact-checking reporter, I will assess the claims made in the text and present a fair perspective to challenge some of the assertions.

1. Taxi Operators Charging More Than Uber: The claim that taxi operators charge 2 to 5 times more than Uber is highly subjective and lacks concrete evidence. Taxi fares vary widely depending on the location, time of day, and other factors. While Uber may have gained popularity for competitive pricing in some instances, it cannot be generalised that taxis always charge significantly more.

2. Uber Bringing Private Rides to the Masses: The

text credits Uber for making private rides available to everyone, but it overlooks the fact that traditional taxi services were already providing private rides to customers for many years before Uber's entry. Uber merely adapted and expanded on an existing service.

3. Uber's Bonuses and Service Fee Changes: The text argues that Uber's reduction in bonuses and increasing service fees are a direct consequence of drivers being treated as workers. However, such business decisions could also be influenced by various other factors, such as market dynamics, operational costs, and competition.

4. Unions for Self-Employed: The text dismisses the idea of unions for self-employed individuals entirely, claiming they are open to corruption. However, unions can play a crucial role in representing the interests of workers and negotiating better working conditions, regardless of their employment status.

5. Uber Altering Online Time: The claim that Uber is intentionally altering online time to deceive drivers and unions is speculative and requires concrete evidence to support it. Without verifiable data, it remains an unfounded accusation.

6. Uber Cannot Force Drivers to Work: The text argues that drivers cannot be forced to work, citing safety concerns. While safety is paramount, this argument ignores the fact that most workers have the

right to refuse work under unsafe conditions, and employers are obligated to provide a safe working environment.

7. Uber Not Providing Tools: The claim that Uber should provide all the tools for drivers to work is unrealistic and not a common practice in the gig economy. Many self-employed individuals typically bear the costs of their tools and equipment.

8. No Contract of Employment with Uber: While it's true that Uber drivers are considered independent contractors, this does not automatically exempt them from certain employment rights. Laws and regulations vary by jurisdiction, and courts have ruled in favor of considering some drivers as workers in certain contexts.

9. Repercussions of Worker Classification: The text emphasises the negative consequences of being classified as a worker without acknowledging potential benefits, such as access to workers' rights and protections.

In conclusion, while the driver expresses strong opinions about Uber and worker classification, their arguments rely heavily on personal beliefs and assumptions. It is essential to consider various perspectives, legal frameworks, and real-world data when analysing the impact of worker classification on drivers and the gig economy as a whole. The situation is complex, and a balanced approach is necessary to address the concerns of all stakeholders involved.

FACT-CHECKING the chapter called:
"The Big Conclusion"

The text provided contains numerous unsubstantiated claims and conspiracy theories that lack credible evidence. As a fact-checking reporter, my role is to challenge these assertions and present a more critical perspective.

1. Blaming the ADCU Founders: The text accuses the founders of the ADCU (App Drivers & Couriers Union) and "others" of being "crooks" with secret affiliations, such as being members of secret societies or undercover government agents. These allegations are baseless and without any evidence. Making unfounded claims about individuals' personal histories is irresponsible and defamatory.

2. Blaming the UK's Courts of Law: Accusing the UK's High Court and The Supreme Court of misinterpreting the workers' law without providing concrete examples or legal analysis is not credible. These courts are staffed by trained and experienced judges who make decisions based on legal principles and precedents.

3. Blaming Uber: The text suggests that Uber had the absolute choice to enforce the decision only on the Plaintiff (ADCU founders) or not at all. However, this

oversimplification overlooks the legal implications and obligations that Uber may have had to address due to the court's ruling.

4. Blaming Transport for London and The Mayor's Office: Accusing TfL and the Mayor of London of openly lobbying against private hire without providing evidence is a baseless claim. Public institutions make decisions based on various factors, including public safety and regulatory concerns.

5. Blaming Drivers: The text criticises drivers who joined the legal action without acknowledging their right to seek legal recourse if they believe their rights have been affected. Making assumptions about these drivers' motives without evidence undermines their right to seek justice.

6. Misunderstanding Supreme Court Decision: The text appears to misunderstand the judicial process and the role of the Supreme Court. The court's response to the author's request indicates a lack of understanding of the legal system.

7. Conspiracy Theories: The text mentions various conspiracy theories, such as the "new world order," "green agenda," and "Agenda 21," without providing any factual basis for these claims. These theories lack credible evidence and are often propagated without any substantive proof.

8. Challenges to Supreme Court Decision: Encouraging all drivers to send similar requests to the Supreme Court and take "Aslam and others" to court for damages appears to be based on a misunderstanding of legal processes. Court decisions are made based on legal arguments and evidence presented during the proceedings, not on mass requests from individuals.

In conclusion, the text contains numerous conspiracy theories and baseless accusations against individuals and institutions. As a fact-checking reporter, I cannot support or validate these claims without credible evidence. It is essential to critically examine information and base conclusions on verifiable facts rather than unfounded speculations or conspiracies. Responsible discourse and decision-making require evidence-based analysis and critical thinking.

My Personal Conclusion

In the final pages of this text, we are presented with a dramatic finale that reads more like a wild conspiracy thriller than a coherent argument. As a fact-checker with a taste for the bizarre, I must say that the claims made here are as fantastical as a unicorn riding a flying saucer.

The author seems to have concocted a perfect recipe for blame, sprinkling allegations of secret societies, government agents, and "the new world order" over a bed of unfounded accusations against individuals and institutions. It's like they raided the pantry of conspiracy theories and threw everything into the pot.

In this literary masterpiece, blame is served generously to the founders of ADCU, the UK's Courts of Law, Uber, Transport for London, The Mayor's Office, and even their fellow drivers, leaving no one spared from the imaginary guilt.

While the author delights in playing the role of an amateur detective, searching for secret affiliations and hidden agendas, they provide not a shred of evidence to back up their wild claims. In this captivating tale of intrigue, they seem to have forgotten that facts are the backbone of any legitimate argument.

In the end, the text reads like a rollercoaster of disbelief, with twists and turns that defy reason. It's as if the author strapped a jetpack to their imagination and soared into the realms of the absurd.

As a fact-checker with a keen eye for the truth, I must conclude that this conclusion is more fiction than fact, and more conspiracy than coherence. So, as you close this book, remember to take everything you've read with a grain of skepticism and a healthy dose of critical thinking. After all, reality is much more fascinating than the wildest of conspiracy theories. Happy fact-checking!

Verdict:

False Information
Missing Context
Clear Intention To Discredit

www.ingramcontent.com/pod-product-compliance
Lightning Source LLC
Chambersburg PA
CBHW051305250726
48656CB00004B/1486